BIBLE
MEMORY
Crosswords

VOLUME 1

BIBLE
MEMORY
Crosswords

100 PUZZLES TO HELP YOU
MEMORIZE SCRIPTURE

BARBOUR BOOKS
An Imprint of Barbour Publishing, Inc.

ISBN 978-1-63409-710-9

Published by Barbour Books, an imprint of Barbour Publishing, Inc., P.O. Box 719, Uhrichsville, Ohio 44683, www.barbourbooks.com

Our mission is to publish and distribute inspirational products offering exceptional value and biblical encouragement to the masses.

ecpa Member of the
Evangelical Christian
Publishers Association

Printed in the United States of America.

WELCOME TO
BIBLE MEMORY CROSSWORDS
VOLUME 1!

The Bible tells us that God's Word illuminates our steps (Psalm 119:105) and that it's quick and powerful and sharper than a two-edged sword (Hebrews 4:12). The Bible is inspired by God (2 Timothy 3:16), and it will endure forever (Isaiah 40:8; Matthew 24:35). In this collection of crossword puzzles, you'll find a brand-new way to memorize scripture (and it just happens to be a whole lot of fun)!

Each puzzle begins with scriptures that include crossword coordinates for several missing words. For example, the missing word where (1D) appears in the scripture will fit into 1 Down on the grid. (4A) means 4 Across, and so forth. Don't know some of the missing words? Try filling in other words in the grid and use the filled-in letters to make a better guess. Entries made up of multiple words include a hint so you know you're looking for more than one word—for example, (3W) means the answer is three words smooshed together in one entry. Still stumped? Answer keys can be found in the back of the book.

Are you up for the challenge? Get ready for the heavenly encouragement of scripture and the fun of word games!

Thy word have I hid in mine heart,
that I might not sin against thee.

PSALM 119:11

1. CREATION PART 1

Genesis 1:1–8

In the (7A) God (14D) the heaven and the (10A). **2** And the earth was without form, and (17D); and darkness was upon the face of the (12A). And the (9A) of God moved upon the face of the waters. **3** And God said, (1A) (2D) (7D) light: and there was light. **4** And God saw the light, that (18A) was (20A): and God divided the (6D) from the (5D). **5** And God (19A) the light Day, and the darkness he called (11D). And the evening and the (15A) were the first day. **6** And God said, Let there be a firmament in the midst of the (8D), and let it divide the waters from the waters. **7** And God made the firmament, and (5A) the waters which were under the firmament from the waters which were above the firmament: and it (3A) so. **8** And God called the firmament (16A). And the (13D) and the morning were the (4D) day.

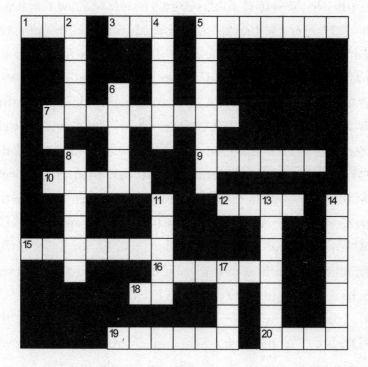

2. CREATION PART 2

Genesis 1:9–19

And God said, Let the waters under the (14D) be gathered together unto one place, and let the (3A) (10D) appear: and it was so. **10** And God called the dry land (6A); and the gathering together of the waters called he (16A): and God saw that it was good. **11** And God said, Let the earth bring forth grass, the herb yielding seed, and the (2A) (8A) yielding fruit after his kind, whose seed is in itself, upon the earth: and (11A/3W). **12** And the earth (5D) (17A) grass, and herb yielding seed after his kind, and the tree (19A) fruit, whose (16D) was in itself, after (18A) (1D): and God saw that it was good. **13** And the (6D) and the morning were the third day. **14** And God said, Let there be lights in the firmament of the heaven to divide the day from the (13A); and let them be for signs, and for (12D), and for days, and years: **15** And let them be for lights in the firmament of the heaven to give light upon the earth: and it was so. **16** And God made two great lights; the greater light to (9A) (4D) day, and the lesser light to rule the night: he made the (7D) also. **17** And God set them in the firmament of the heaven to give light upon the earth, **18** And to rule over the day and over the night, and to divide the light from the darkness: and God saw that (15A/3W). **19** And the evening and the morning were the (2D) day.

3. CREATION PART 3

Genesis 1:20–25

And God said, Let the waters bring forth abundantly the moving creature that hath (12A), and (11A) that may fly above the (13D) in the open firmament of (9A). **21** And God created great (2D), and every living creature that moveth, which the (10D) brought forth abundantly, after their kind, and every (2A) fowl after his kind: and God saw that it was good. **22** And God (14A) them, saying, Be fruitful, and (7A), and fill the waters in the seas, and let fowl multiply in the earth. **23** And the evening and the morning were the fifth (8A). **24** And God said, Let the earth bring forth the (4A) (3D) after his kind, cattle, and creeping thing, and beast of the earth after his kind: and it was so. **25** And God made the (1D) of the earth after his kind, and (6A) after their kind, and every thing that (3A) upon the earth (15A/3W): and God saw that (5D/3W).

4. CREATION PART 4

Genesis 1:26–29, 31; 2:1–3

And God said, Let us make man in our (1A), after our likeness: and let them have (18A) over the fish of the (5A), and over the fowl of the (2D), and over the (9D), and over all the earth, and over every creeping thing that (3D) upon the (19A). **27** So God created man in his own image, in the (8D) of God created he him; male and female created he them. **28** And God blessed them, and God said unto them, Be (11D), and multiply, and (12A) the earth, and subdue it: and have dominion over the (16D) of the sea, and over the fowl of the air, and over every living thing that moveth upon the earth. **29** And God said, Behold, I have given you every herb bearing (14A), which is upon the face of all the earth, and every tree, in the which is the (17A) of a tree yielding seed; to you it shall be for meat. . . . **31** And God saw every thing that he had made, and, behold, it was very good. And the (10A) and the morning were the (15A) day. . . . **1** Thus the (4D) and the earth were finished, and all the host of them. **2** And on the (13D) day God ended his work which he had made; and he (6A) on the seventh day from all his work which he had made. **3** And God blessed the seventh day, and (7D) it: because that in it he had rested from all his work which God created and made.

5. ADAM

Genesis 2:7–17

And the Lord God (13D) man of the dust of the ground, and breathed into his nostrils the breath of life; and man became a living soul. **8** And the Lord God planted a garden eastward in (12A); and there he put the man whom he had formed. **9** And out of the ground made the Lord God to grow every tree that is pleasant to the sight, and good for (15D); the (6D) of life also in the midst of the garden, and the tree of (9A) of good and evil. **10** And a (8A) went out of Eden to water the garden; and from thence it was parted, and became into (4D) heads. **11** The name of the first is (14D): that is it which compasseth the whole land of (3D), where there is gold; **12** And the gold of that land is good: there is bdellium and the onyx stone. **13** And the name of the second river is (2A): the same is it that compasseth the whole land of Ethiopia. **14** And the name of the third river is (1D): that is it which goeth toward the east of Assyria. And the fourth river is (16A). **15** And the Lord God took the man, and put him into the (18A) of Eden to dress it and to keep it. **16** And the Lord God (7D) the man, saying, Of every tree of the garden thou mayest freely (5A): **17** But of the tree of the knowledge of (17A) and (11A), thou shalt not eat of it: for in the day that thou eatest thereof thou shalt surely (10D).

6. EVE

Genesis 2:18-25

And the LORD God said, It is not good that the man should (16A/2W); I will make him an help meet for him. **19** And out of the ground the LORD God formed every beast of the (12A), and every (8A) of the air; and brought them unto (15D) to see what he would call them: and whatsoever Adam called every living (6A), that was the name thereof. **20** And Adam gave names to all (6D), and to the fowl of the air, and to every beast of the field; but for Adam there was not found an (7A/2W) for him. **21** And the LORD God caused a deep (4D) to fall upon Adam, and he slept: and he took one of his (14D), and closed up the flesh instead thereof; **22** And the rib, which the LORD God had taken from man, made he a woman, and (2A) her unto the man. **23** And Adam said, This is now bone of my (9A), and flesh of my (5D): she shall be called Woman, because she was taken out of Man. **24** Therefore shall a man leave his (13A) and his (1D), and shall cleave unto his (11D): and they shall be (3D/2W). **25** And they were both (10D), the man and his wife, and were not (15A).

7. THE TEMPTATION OF EVE

Genesis 3:1–8

Now the serpent was more subtil than any (3D) of the field which the LORD God had made. And he said unto the (17A), Yea, hath God said, Ye shall not eat of every tree of the (5D)? **2** And the woman said unto the (2D), We may eat of the (15D) of the (12A) of the garden: **3** But of the fruit of the tree which is in the midst of the garden, God hath said, Ye shall not (7D) of it, neither shall ye (18A) it, lest ye die. **4** And the serpent said unto the woman, Ye shall not (6A/2W): **5** For God doth know that in the day ye eat thereof, then your eyes shall be (19A), and ye shall be as gods, knowing (14D) and (13D). **6** And when the woman saw that the tree was good for food, and that it was (10D) to the eyes, and a tree to be desired to make one (11D), she took of the fruit thereof, and did eat, and gave also unto her (1A) with her; and he did eat. **7** And the (13A) of them both were opened, and they knew that they were (9D); and they sewed (4A) leaves together, and made themselves aprons. **8** And they heard the voice of the LORD God walking in the garden in the (16D) of the day: and Adam and his wife hid themselves from the (8A) of the LORD God amongst the trees of the garden.

8. NOAH AND THE ARK

Genesis 6:13–22

And God said unto (5D), The end of all flesh is come before me; for the earth is filled with (1D) through them; and, behold, I will (14D) them with the earth. **14** Make thee an ark of (19A/2W); rooms shalt thou make in the ark, and shalt pitch it within and without with pitch. **15** And this is the fashion which thou shalt make it of: The (3D) of the ark shall be three hundred cubits, the (15A) of it fifty (7D), and the (11A) of it thirty cubits. **16** A window shalt thou make to the ark, and in a cubit shalt thou finish it above; and the door of the ark shalt thou set in the side thereof; with lower, second, and (16D) stories shalt thou make it. **17** And, behold, I, even I, do bring a flood of waters upon the earth, to destroy all flesh, wherein is the (9A) of life, from under heaven; and every thing that is in the earth (17A) (14A). **18** But with thee will I establish my (2D); and thou shalt come into the (18D), thou, and thy sons, and thy (4D), and thy sons' wives with thee. **19** And of every (8A) (6D) of all flesh, (13A) of every sort shalt thou bring into the ark, to keep them alive with thee; they shall be male and (12D). **20** Of fowls after their kind, and of cattle after their kind, of every creeping thing of the earth after his kind, two of every sort shall come unto thee, to keep them (10D). **21** And take thou unto thee of all food that is eaten, and thou shalt gather it to thee; and it shall be for food for thee, and for them. **22** Thus did Noah; according to all that God commanded him, so did he.

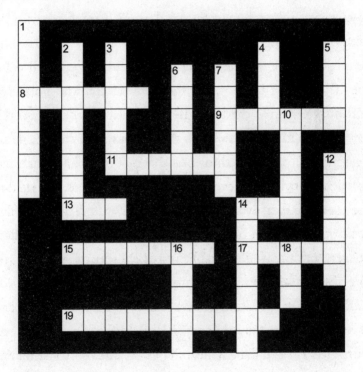

9. THE PROMISE

Genesis 8:1, 15–22

And God remembered (1D), and every living thing, and all the cattle that was with him in the ark. . . . **15** And God (17D) unto Noah, saying, **16** Go forth of the ark, thou, and thy wife, and thy sons, and thy sons' wives with thee. **17** Bring forth with thee every living thing that is with thee, of all flesh, both of fowl, and of cattle, and of every creeping thing that (4D) upon the earth; that they may (9A) abundantly in the earth, and be fruitful, and multiply upon the (8A). **18** And Noah went forth, and his (18D), and his (3D), and his sons' wives with him: **19** Every beast, every creeping thing, and every fowl, and whatsoever creepeth upon the earth, after their kinds, went forth (12A) of the (6A). **20** And Noah builded an (15D) unto the Lord; and took of every clean beast, and of every clean fowl, and offered burnt (16A) on the altar. **21** And the Lord smelled a (10A) (19A); and the Lord said in his heart, I will not again (5D) the ground any more for man's sake; for the (2D) of man's heart is evil from his youth; neither will I again (20A) any more every thing living, as I have done. **22** While the earth remaineth, seedtime and (7D), and cold and (14A), and summer and (11D), and day and (13A) shall not cease.

10. GOD'S COVENANT WITH ABRAM

Genesis 12:1–3; 15:18–21

Now the LORD had said unto (5A), Get thee out of thy (10D), and from thy kindred, and from thy father's (7D), unto a land that I will shew thee: **2** And I will make of thee a great (9A), and I will (12D) thee, and make thy name (14A); and thou shalt be a blessing: **3** And I will bless them that bless thee, and (1A) him that (3D) thee: and in thee shall all (2D) of the earth be blessed. . . . **18** In the same day the (11A) made a (1D) with Abram, saying, Unto thy seed have I given this (4D), from the river of Egypt unto the great river, the river (6A): **19** The (13A), and the (8D), and the Kadmonites, **20** And the Hittites, and the Perizzites, and the (15A), **21** And the (5D), and the Canaanites, and the Girgashites, and the Jebusites.

11. ABRAHAM AND ISAAC

Genesis 22:1–2. 6–13

And it (19A) to (12A) after these things, that God did tempt Abraham, and said unto him, Abraham: and he said, Behold, here I am. **2** And he said, Take now thy son, thine only son (3D), whom thou (13D), and get thee into the land of (16A); and offer him there for a burnt offering upon one of the (4A) which I will tell thee of. . . . **6** And Abraham took the wood of the (1D) (9D), and laid it upon Isaac his son; and he took the fire in his hand, and a knife; and they went both of them together. **7** And Isaac spake unto Abraham his father, and said, (4D) (11D): and he said, Here am I, my son. And he said, Behold the fire and the (8A): but where is the lamb for a burnt offering? **8** And Abraham said, My son, God will (12D) himself a lamb for a burnt offering: so they went both of them (10A). **9** And they came to the place which God had told him of; and Abraham built an (15D) there, and laid the wood in order, and bound Isaac his son, and laid him on the altar upon the wood. **10** And Abraham stretched forth his hand, and took the (14D) to slay his son. **11** And the (5A) of the (6D) called unto him out of (17A), and said, Abraham, Abraham: and he said, Here am I. **12** And he said, Lay not thine hand upon the lad, neither do thou any thing unto him: for now I know that thou (18A) God, seeing thou hast not withheld thy son, thine only son from me. **13** And Abraham lifted up his (7D), and looked, and behold behind him a ram

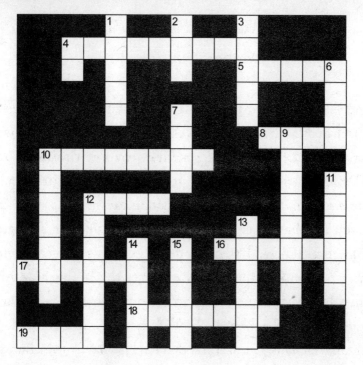

caught in a (10D) by his horns: and Abraham went and took the (2D), and offered him up for a burnt offering in the stead of his son.

12. JACOB AND ESAU
Genesis 25:21–34

And Isaac intreated the LORD for his wife, because she was (19A): and the LORD was (20A) of him, and Rebekah his wife conceived. **22** And the children (6A) together within her; and she said, If it be so, why am I thus? And she went to enquire of the LORD. **23** And the LORD said unto her, (13D) (4A) are in thy womb, and two manner of people shall be separated from thy (3D); and the one people shall be (8A) than the other people; and the elder shall serve the younger. **24** And when her days to be delivered were fulfilled, behold, there were (14D) in her womb. **25** And the first came out red, all over like an hairy (7D); and they called his name (9A). **26** And after that came his brother out, and his hand took hold on Esau's (18D); and his name was called (5A): and Isaac was threescore years old when she bare them. **27** And the boys grew: and Esau was a cunning hunter, a man of the field; and Jacob was a plain man, dwelling in (12A). **28** And Isaac loved Esau, because he did eat of his (10D): but (11A) loved Jacob. **29** And Jacob sod pottage: and Esau came from the field, and he was faint: **30** And Esau said to Jacob, (17D) me, I pray thee, with that same red pottage; for I am (16D): therefore was his name called Edom. **31** And Jacob said, Sell me this day thy (15A). **32** And Esau said, Behold, I am at the point to die: and what (2D) shall this birthright do to me? **33** And Jacob said, Swear to me this day; and he sware unto him: and he sold

his birthright unto Jacob. **34** Then Jacob gave Esau bread and pottage of (21A); and he did eat and drink, and rose up, and went his way: thus Esau (1A) his birthright.

13. MOSES IN THE BASKET

Exodus 2:1–10

And there went a man of the (9A) of (8D), and took to wife a daughter of Levi. **2** And the woman conceived, and (18D) a son: and when she saw him that he was a (1A) child, she hid him (10A) (15D). **3** And when she could not longer hide him, she took for him an ark of bulrushes, and daubed it with slime and with (16D), and put the child therein; and she laid it in the flags by the river's brink. **4** And his (14D) stood afar off, to wit what would be done to him. **5** And the daughter of (20A) came down to (7D) (6A) at the river; and her maidens walked along by the river's side; and when she saw the ark among the flags, she sent her (12D) to fetch it. **6** And when she had opened it, she saw the (17A): and, behold, the babe wept. And she had compassion on him, and said, This is one of the Hebrews' (19A). **7** Then said his sister to Pharaoh's (3D), Shall I go and call to thee a nurse of the (4D) women, that she may nurse the child for thee? **8** And Pharaoh's daughter said to her, Go. And the maid went and called the child's mother. **9** And Pharaoh's daughter said unto her, Take this child away, and nurse it for me, and I will give thee thy wages. And the women took the child, and (13D) it. **10** And the child (1D), and she brought him unto Pharaoh's daughter, and he (5A) her son. And she called his name Moses: and she said, Because I (2D) (11A) out of the water.

14. MOSES AND THE BURNING BUSH

Exodus 3:1–8

Now Moses kept the flock of Jethro his (1D) in (10A), the priest of (9D): and he led the (5A) to the backside of the desert, and came to the (15A) of God, even to Horeb. **2** And the (13D) of the LORD appeared unto him in a flame of fire out of the midst of a (4D): and he looked, and, behold, the bush burned with (1A), and the bush was not consumed. **3** And (16A) said, I will now turn aside, and see this great sight, why the bush is not burnt. **4** And when the LORD saw that he turned aside to see, God called unto him out of the midst of the bush, and said, Moses, Moses. And he said, Here am I. **5** And he said, Draw not nigh hither: put off thy (2A) from off thy feet, for the place whereon thou standest is (3D) (14D). **6** Moreover he said, I am the God of thy father, the God of (8A), the God of (11A), and the God of (7D). And Moses hid his (17D); for he was afraid to look upon God. **7** And the LORD said, I have surely seen the (18A) of my people which are in (19A), and have heard their cry by reason of their taskmasters; for I know their sorrows; **8** And I am come down to deliver them out of the hand of the Egyptians, and to bring them up out of that land unto a good land and a large, unto a land flowing with milk and (12A); unto the place of the (6D), and the Hittites, and the Amorites, and the Perizzites, and the Hivites, and the Jebusites.

15. THE CROSSING OF THE RED SEA

Exodus 14:21–23, 26–31

And Moses stretched out his hand over the sea; and the LORD caused the sea to go back by a strong (11D) wind all that night, and made the sea (14A) land, and the waters were divided. **22** And the children of Israel went into the midst of the sea upon the dry (8A): and the waters were a wall unto them on their right hand, and on their (19A). **23** And the Egyptians pursued, and went in after them to the midst of the sea, even all Pharaoh's horses, his (3D), and his (18A). . . . **26** And the LORD said unto (16D), Stretch out thine hand over the sea, that the waters may come again upon the (7D), upon their chariots, and upon their horsemen. **27** And Moses stretched forth his hand over the sea, and the sea returned to his strength when the (13D) appeared; and the Egyptians fled against it; and the LORD (2D) the Egyptians in the midst of the sea. **28** And the waters returned, and (5A) the chariots, and the horsemen, and all the host of (9A) that came into the sea after them; there remained not so much as one of them. **29** But the children of (6D) walked upon dry land in the midst of the sea; and the waters were a wall unto them on their (15D) hand, and on their left. **30** Thus the LORD (17A) Israel that day out of the (12D) of the Egyptians; and Israel saw the Egyptians dead upon the (10A/2W). **31** And Israel saw that great work which the LORD did upon the Egyptians: and the people (1D) the LORD, and (4A) the LORD, and his servant Moses.

16. SAMUEL'S CALLING

1 Samuel 3:2–11, 19–21

And it came to pass at that time, when Eli was laid down in his place, and his eyes began to (15A) (4D), that he could not see; **3** And ere the (16D) of God went out in the (18A) of the LORD, where the ark of God was, and Samuel was laid down to sleep; **4** That the LORD called (7A): and he answered, Here am I. **5** And he ran unto Eli, and said, (9D) am I; for thou calledst me. And he said, I called not; lie down again. And he went and (17A) down. **6** And the LORD called yet again, Samuel. And Samuel (5A) and went to Eli, and said, Here am I; for thou didst call me. And he answered, I called not, my son; lie down again. **7** Now Samuel did not yet know the LORD, neither was the word of the LORD yet (10D) unto him. **8** And the LORD called Samuel again the (14A) time. And he arose and went to Eli, and said, Here am I; for thou didst call me. And Eli (3D) that the LORD had called the child. **9** Therefore Eli said unto Samuel, Go, lie down: and it shall be, if he call thee, that thou shalt say, (19A), LORD; for thy (1D) heareth. So Samuel went and lay down in his place. **10** And the LORD came, and stood, and called as at other times, Samuel, Samuel. Then Samuel answered, Speak; for thy servant (6D). **11** And the LORD said to Samuel, Behold, I will do a thing in Israel, at which both the ears of every one that heareth it shall (11D). . . . **19** And Samuel (12A), and the LORD was with him, and did let none of his words fall to the ground. **20** And all Israel from Dan even to (2D) knew that

Samuel was established to be a (3A) of the LORD. **21** And the LORD appeared again in (8A): for the LORD revealed himself to Samuel in Shiloh by the (13D) of the (16A).

17. DAVID AND GOLIATH

1 Samuel 17:45–51

Then said David to the (4D), Thou comest to me with a (10A), and with a spear, and with a shield: but I come to thee in the name of the LORD of hosts, the God of the armies of (3D), whom thou hast (2A). **46** This day will the LORD (11D) thee into mine hand; and I will (8D) (17A), and take thine head from thee; and I will give the carcases of the host of the Philistines this day unto the fowls of the air, and to the wild beasts of the earth; that all the earth may know that there is a God in Israel. **47** And all this (7A) shall know that the LORD saveth not with sword and (19A): for the battle is the LORD's, and he will give you (1D) our (14D). **48** And it came to pass, when the Philistine arose, and came, and drew nigh to meet David, that David hastened, and ran toward the (15A) to meet the Philistine. **49** And David put his hand in his bag, and took thence a (9A), and slang it, and smote the Philistine in his forehead, that the stone sunk into his (12D); and he fell upon his face to the earth. **50** So David prevailed over the Philistine with a (13A) and with a stone, and smote the Philistine, and slew him; but there was no sword in the hand of David. **51** Therefore David ran, and stood upon the Philistine, and took his sword, and drew it out of the (5A) thereof, and slew him, and (6D/2W) his (18D) therewith. And when the Philistines saw their (16A) was (20A), they fled.

18. DANIEL AND THE LIONS' DEN

Daniel 6:16–23, 28

Then the king commanded, and they brought Daniel, and cast him into the (9A) of (6A). Now the king spake and said unto Daniel, Thy God whom thou servest continually, he will (12D) (13A). **17** And a (2D) was brought, and laid upon the mouth of the den; and the king sealed it with his own (4D), and with the signet of his lords; that the purpose might not be changed concerning Daniel. **18** Then the king went to his (5A), and passed the night (3D): neither were (15A) of musick brought before him: and his sleep went from him. **19** Then the king arose very early in the (10A), and went in haste unto the den of lions. **20** And when he came to the den, he cried with a lamentable voice unto Daniel: and the king spake and said to (14D), O Daniel, servant of the living God, is thy God, whom thou servest continually, able to deliver thee from the lions? **21** Then said Daniel unto the king, O king, (16D) (7D/2W). **22** My God hath sent his angel, and hath shut the lions' (8D), that they have not hurt me: forasmuch as before him innocency was found in me; and also before thee, O king, have I done no hurt. **23** Then was the king (18A) (17D) for him, and commanded that they should take Daniel up out of the den. So Daniel was taken up out of the den, and no manner of hurt was found upon him, because he (11D) in his God. . . . **28** So this Daniel (1A) in the reign of (19A), and in the reign of Cyrus the Persian.

19. THE TOWER OF BABEL

Genesis 11:1–9

And the whole earth was of one (6A), and of one speech. 2 And it (13A) to (9A), as they journeyed from the east, that they found a plain in the land of (11A); and they dwelt there. 3 And they said one to (4D), Go to, let us make (17A), and burn them thoroughly. And they had brick for stone, and slime had they for morter. 4 And they said, Go to, let us (1D) us a city and a (16A), whose top may reach unto (3D); and let us make us a name, lest we be scattered abroad upon the face of the whole (14D). 5 And the LORD came down to see the (7A) and the tower, which the children of (8A) builded. 6 And the LORD said, Behold, the people is one, and they have all one language; and this they begin to do: and now nothing will be restrained from them, which they have (12D) to do. 7 Go to, let us go down, and there (5A) their language, that they may not understand one another's (18A). 8 So the LORD (10D) them abroad from thence upon the (2D) of all the earth: and they left off to build the city. 9 Therefore is the name of it called (1A); because the LORD did there confound the language of all the earth: and from thence did the LORD scatter them (15A) upon the face of all the earth.

20. JACOB'S LADDER

Genesis 28:10–13, 15–16, 18–22

And Jacob went out from (10D), and went toward Haran. **11** And he lighted upon a certain place, and tarried there all night, because the sun was set; and he took of the stones of that place, and put them for his pillows, and lay down in that place to sleep. **12** And he (14D), and behold a (13A) set up on the earth, and the top of it reached to (8D): and behold the (2D) of God ascending and (3A) on it. **13** And, behold, the LORD stood above it, and said, I am the LORD God of (6D) thy father, and the God of (1D): the land whereon thou liest, to thee will I give it, and to thy seed; . . . . **15** And, behold, (17A/2W) with (16A), and will keep thee in all places whither thou goest, and will bring thee again into this land; for I will not leave thee, until I have done that which I have spoken to thee of. **16** And (18A) awaked out of his (4D), and he said, Surely the LORD is in this (5A); and I knew it not. . . . **18** And Jacob rose up early in the morning, and took the stone that he had put for his pillows, and set it up for a pillar, and poured oil upon the top of it. **19** And he called the name of that place (11A): but the name of that city was called Luz at the first. **20** And Jacob (19A) a vow, saying, If God will be with me, and will keep me in this way that I go, and will give me (10A) to (7A), and raiment to put on, **21** So that I come again to my father's house in (15D); then shall the LORD (11D/3W): **22** And this stone, which I have set for a (9A), shall be God's house: and of all that thou shalt give me I will surely give the (12D) unto thee.

21. DAVID CHOSEN BY GOD

1 Samuel 16:1–13

And the Lord said unto Samuel, How long wilt thou mourn for Saul, seeing I have rejected him from (7D) over Israel? fill thine (15D) with (14A), and go, I will send thee to Jesse the Bethlehemite: for I have provided me a king among his sons.... 6 And it came to pass, when they were come, that he looked on Eliab, and said, Surely the Lord's (11D) is before him. 7 But the Lord said unto (13D), Look not on his countenance, or on the (8D) of his stature; because I have (1D) him: for the Lord seeth not as man seeth; for man looketh on the (4D) appearance, but the Lord looketh on the (5D). 8 Then Jesse called Abinadab, and made him pass before Samuel. And he said, Neither hath the (16A) chosen this. 9 Then Jesse made Shammah to pass by. And he said, Neither hath the Lord (12A) this. 10 Again, Jesse made seven of his (3A) to pass before Samuel. And Samuel said unto Jesse, The Lord hath not chosen these. 11 And Samuel said unto Jesse, Are here all thy (10D)? And he said, There remaineth yet the (17A), and, behold, he keepeth the sheep. And Samuel said unto Jesse, Send and (2A) (5A): for we will not sit down till he come hither. 12 And he sent, and brought him in. Now he was ruddy, and withal of a beautiful (18A), and goodly to look to. And the Lord said, Arise, (9A) him: for this is he. 13 Then Samuel took the horn of oil, and anointed him in the midst of his brethren: and the (6A) of the Lord came upon David from that day forward.

22. THE BATTLE OF JERICHO

Joshua 6:12–16, 20–21

And Joshua rose early in the morning, and the priests took up the ark of the LORD. **13** And seven (13A) bearing (5D) (18A) of rams' horns before the (3D) of the (15A) went on continually, and (6D) with the trumpets: and the armed men went before them; but the rereward came after the ark of the LORD, the priests going on, and (6A) with the trumpets. **14** And the second day they compassed the city once, and returned into the camp: so they did six days. **15** And it came to pass on the (10D) day, that they (4A) early about the dawning of the day, and (1A) the city after the same manner seven times: only on that day they compassed the city seven times. **16** And it came to pass at the seventh time, when the priests blew with the trumpets, (17A) said unto the people, (12D); for the LORD hath given you the city. . . . **20** So the people (14D) when the priests blew with the trumpets: and it (1D) to pass, when the people heard the sound of the trumpet, and the people shouted with a (11D) (16D), that the wall (9D) (2D) (9A), so that the (19A) went up into the city, every man straight before him, and they took the city. **21** And they (7D) (8A) all that was in the city.

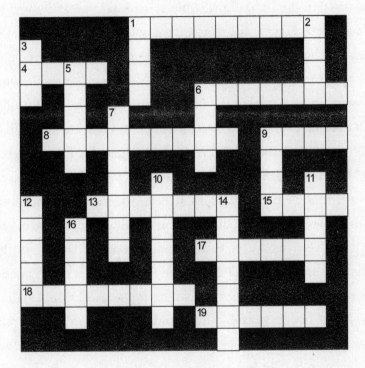

23. SHADRACH, MESHACH, AND ABEDNEGO

Daniel 3:14-25

Nebuchadnezzar spake and said unto them, Is it true, O Shadrach, Meshach, and Abednego, do not ye serve my gods, nor worship the (9A) (15A) which I have set up? **15** Now if ye be ready that at what time ye hear the sound of the cornet, (8D), harp, sackbut, psaltery, and dulcimer, and all kinds of musick, ye fall down and (17A) the image which I have made; well: but if ye worship not, ye shall be cast the same hour into the midst of a burning (18A) (16A); and who is that God that shall (5D) you out of my hands? **16** (19A), Meshach, and (1D), answered and said to the king, O Nebuchadnezzar, we are not careful to answer thee in this matter. **17** If it be so, our God whom we (10D) is able to deliver us from the burning fiery furnace, and he will deliver us out of thine hand, O king. **18** But if not, be it known unto thee, (2D/2W), that we will not serve thy gods, nor worship the golden image which thou hast set up. **19** Then was Nebuchadnezzar full of fury, and the form of his visage was changed against Shadrach, Meshach, and Abednego: therefore he spake, and commanded that they should heat the furnace one (10A) times more than it was wont to be heated. **20** And he (11D) the most (14D) men that were in his army to bind Shadrach, Meshach, and Abednego, and to cast them into the burning fiery furnace. **21** Then these men were bound in their coats, their hosen, and their hats, and their other (4D), and were

cast into the midst of the burning fiery furnace. . . . **24** Then Nebuchadnezzar the king was astonished, and rose up in haste, and spake, and said unto his (12A), Did not we cast (3D) (14A) bound into the midst of the fire? They answered and said unto the king, (6A), O king. **25** He answered and said, Lo, I see four men loose, walking in the midst of the fire, and they have no hurt; and the form of the fourth is like the (13D) of (7A).

24. JOSEPH'S COAT OF MANY COLORS

Genesis 37:3–34

Now (2D) loved Joseph more than all his (19A), because he was the son of his old age: and he made him a coat of many colours. **4** And when his brethren saw that their (13D) loved him more than all his brethren, they (17A) (9A), and could not speak (10A) unto him. **5** And Joseph (3D) a dream, and he told it his brethren: and they hated him yet the more. . . . **17** And Joseph went after his (11D), and found them in (7D). **18** And when they saw him afar off, even before he came near unto them, they (5A) against him to slay him. . . . **23** And it came to pass, when (15A) was come unto his brethren, that they stript Joseph out of his coat, his coat of many colours that was on him; **24** And they took him, and cast him (12A) a (6D): and the pit was empty, there was no (8A) in it. . . . **28** Then there passed by Midianites merchantmen; and they drew and lifted up Joseph out of the pit, and sold Joseph to the Ishmeelites for twenty pieces of (1A): and they brought Joseph into (18A). . . . **31** And they took Joseph's coat, and killed a kid of the (14D), and dipped the coat in the blood; **32** And they sent the coat of many colours, and they brought it to their father; and said, This have we found: know now whether it be thy son's coat or no. **33** And he knew it, and said, It is my son's coat; an (16D) beast hath devoured him; Joseph is without doubt rent in pieces. **34** And Jacob rent his clothes, and put sackcloth upon his loins, and (4D) for his son many days.

25. THE GOLDEN CALF

Exodus 32:7-8, 15-20

And the LORD said unto Moses, Go, get thee down; for thy (4D), which thou broughtest out of the land of (1A), have corrupted themselves: 8 They have turned aside quickly out of the way which I (7D) them: they have made them a molten (15D), and have worshipped it, and have sacrificed thereunto, and said, These be thy gods, O Israel, which have brought thee up out of the land of Egypt. . . . 15 And (9A) turned, and went down from the (16A), and the two tables of the (12A) were in his hand: the (2D) were written on both their sides; on the one side and on the other were they (5D). 16 And the tables were the work of God, and the writing was the writing of God, (17A) upon the tables. 17 And when Joshua heard the noise of the people as they shouted, he said unto Moses, There is a (14D) of (5A) in the camp. 18 And he said, It is not the voice of them that shout for mastery, neither is it the voice of them that cry for being (18A): but the noise of them that sing do I hear. 19 And it came to pass, as soon as he came nigh unto the (3A), that he saw the calf, and the (11D): and Moses' anger (10A) hot, and he cast the tables out of his (8D), and brake them beneath the mount. 20 And he took the calf which they had made, and burnt it in the fire, and ground it to (6A), and strawed it upon the water, and made the children of Israel (13A) of it.

26. THE PROMISE OF ISAAC

Genesis 17:1-9, 15-19

And when Abram was ninety years old and nine, the LORD appeared to (2D), and said unto him, I am the (13A) (14D); walk before me, and be thou (8A). **2** And I will make my (5D) between me and thee, and will (7D) thee exceedingly. **3** And Abram fell on his face: and God talked with him, saying, **4** As for me, behold, my covenant is with thee, and thou shalt be a father of many (11D). **5** Neither shall thy name any more be called Abram, but thy name shall be Abraham; for a father of many nations have I made thee. **6** And I will make thee (1D) fruitful, and I will make nations of thee, and (15A) shall come out of thee. **7** And I will establish my covenant (3D) me and thee and thy seed after thee in their generations for an (1A) covenant, to be a God unto thee, and to thy seed after thee. **8** And I will give unto thee, and to thy seed after thee, the land wherein thou art a (6D), all the land of Canaan, for an everlasting possession; and I will be their God. **9** And God said unto Abraham, Thou shalt keep my covenant therefore, thou, and thy seed after thee in their (10A).... **15** And God said unto Abraham, As for Sarai thy wife, thou shalt not call her name Sarai, but (4A) shall her name be. **16** And I will bless her, and give thee a son also of her: yea, I will bless her, and she shall be a (12D) of nations; kings of people shall be of her. **17** Then Abraham fell upon his face, and laughed, and said in his heart, Shall a child be born unto him that is an (16A) years old? and

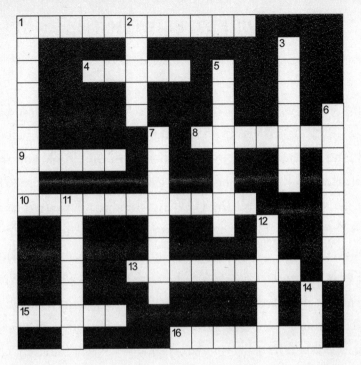

shall Sarah, that is ninety years old, bear? **18** And Abraham said unto God, O that Ishmael might live before thee! **19** And God said, Sarah thy wife shall bear thee a son indeed; and thou shalt call his name (9A): and I will establish my covenant with him for an everlasting covenant, and with his seed after him.

27. JACOB WRESTLES WITH THE ANGEL

Genesis 32:22-31

And [Jacob] rose up that (17A), and took his two wives, and his two (2D), and his eleven sons, and passed over the ford Jabbok. **23** And he took them, and sent them over the brook, and sent over that he had. **24** And (4A) was left alone; and there (8D) a man with him until the (11D) of the day. **25** And when he saw that he (15A) not against him, he touched the hollow of his (5A); and the hollow of Jacob's thigh was out of (1D), as he wrestled with him. **26** And he said, (13A/3W), for the day breaketh. And he said, I will not let thee go, except thou (11A) me. **27** And he said unto him, What is thy (12D)? And he said, Jacob. **28** And he said, Thy name shall be called no more Jacob, but (7D): for as a prince hast thou (9A) with God and with (14A), and hast prevailed. **29** And Jacob (10A) him, and said, Tell me, I pray (5D), thy name. And he said, Wherefore is it that thou dost ask after my name? And he blessed him there. **30** And Jacob called the name of the place (6A): for I have seen God face to (3D), and my life is (9D). **31** And as he passed over Penuel the (16A) rose upon him, and he halted upon his thigh.

28. ELIJAH AND BAAL

1 Kings 18:31-39

And Elijah took twelve (2D), according to the number of the tribes of the (10A) of (6D), unto whom the word of the LORD came, saying, Israel shall be thy name: **32** And with the stones he built an (11A) in the name of the LORD: and he made a (14D) about the altar, as great as would contain two measures of seed. **33** And he put the wood in order, and cut the (12A) in pieces, and laid him on the wood, and said, Fill four (5D) with water, and pour it on the burnt (10D), and on the wood. **34** And he said, Do it the second time. And they did it the second time. And he said, Do it the third time. And they did it the (16A) time. **35** And the water ran round about the altar; and he filled the trench also with (19A). **36** And it (1D) to pass at the time of the offering of the evening sacrifice, that (17A) the (13D) came near, and said, LORD God of Abraham, (8A), and of Israel, let it be known this day that thou art God in (4D), and that I am thy (9D), and that I have done all these things at thy word. **37** (18A/2W), O LORD, hear me, that this people may know that thou art the LORD God, and that thou hast turned their heart back again. **38** Then the (3A) of the LORD fell, and consumed the burnt sacrifice, and the wood, and the stones, and the dust, and (15D) up the water that was in the trench. **39** And when all the people saw it, they fell on their (7A): and they said, The LORD, he is the God; the LORD, he is the God.

29. RAHAB AND THE SPIES

Joshua 2:1, 3-4, 6, 15-21

And Joshua the (19D) of (20A) sent out of Shittim two men to (15A) secretly, saying, Go view the land, even (11D). And they went, and came into an harlot's house, named Rahab, and lodged there. . . . **3** And the king of Jericho sent unto Rahab, saying, Bring forth the men that are come to thee, which are entered into thine (16D): for they be come to search out all the (10D). **4** And the woman took the (6D) (9A), and hid them. . . . **6** But she had brought them up to the (17D) of the house, and hid them with the stalks of (3D), which she had laid in order upon the roof. . . . **15** Then she let them down by a cord through the (7A): for her house was upon the town (4A), and she dwelt upon the wall. **16** And she said unto them, Get you to the (12D), lest the pursuers meet you; and hide yourselves there three (13A), until the pursuers be returned: and afterward may ye go your way. **17** And the men said unto her. . . **18** Behold, when we come into the land, thou shalt bind this line of (5A) thread in the window which thou didst let us down by: and thou shalt bring thy (21A), and thy mother, and thy brethren, and all thy father's (14A), home unto thee. **19** And it shall be, that whosoever shall go out of the (18A) of thy house into the street, his (1D) shall be upon his head, and we will be guiltless: and whosoever shall be with thee in the house, his blood shall be on our head, if any hand be upon him. **20** And if thou utter

this our (2D), then we will be quit of thine oath which thou hast made us to swear. **21** And she said, According unto your (8D), so be it. And she sent them away, and they departed: and she bound the scarlet line in the window.

30. THE CROSSING OF THE JORDAN

Joshua 3:5, 14–17

And Joshua said unto the people, (9A) yourselves: for to morrow the LORD will do wonders among you. . . . **14** And it (20A) to (6D), when the people removed from their (7A), to pass over Jordan, and the priests bearing the ark of the (11D) before the people; **15** And as they that bare the ark were come unto (16A), and the feet of the (3A) that bare the ark were dipped in the brim of the (12D), (for Jordan overfloweth all his banks all the time of (17A),) **16** That the waters which came down from (13A) stood and rose up upon an heap very far from the city (18D), that is beside Zaretan: and those that came down toward the sea of the plain, even the (14A) (19D), failed, and were cut off: and the people (4D) over right against (5D). **17** And the priests that bare the (10D) of the covenant of the (15D) stood firm on (1D) ground in the midst of Jordan, and all the (2D) passed over on dry ground, until all the people were passed (8A) over Jordan.

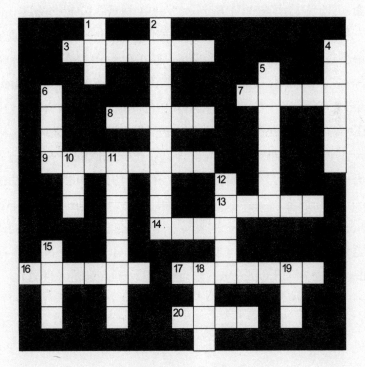

31. MANNA AND QUAIL FROM HEAVEN

Exodus 16:4, 11–15

Then said the LORD unto Moses, Behold, I will (13D) bread from (10D) for you; and the people shall go out and gather a certain rate (15A) (17A), that I may prove them, whether they will walk in (14D/2W), or no. . . . **11** And the LORD spake unto (19A), saying, **12** I have heard the (3D) of the children of (12A): speak unto them, saying, At even ye shall eat (11A), and in the morning ye shall be filled with (1A); and ye shall know that I am the (5A) your God. **13** And it (2A) to (6A), that at even the (4D) came up, and covered the camp: and in the morning the dew lay round about the host. **14** And when the (8A) that lay was gone up, (1D), upon the face of the (9D) there lay a small round thing, as small as the hoar frost on the ground. **15** And when the children of Israel saw it, they said one to (18A), It is (7A): for they wist not what it was. And Moses said unto them, This is the bread which the LORD hath given you to (16D).

32. ELIJAH AND THE WIDOW

1 Kings 17:7–16

And it came to pass after a while, that the (19A) dried up, because there had been no rain in the (4D). **8** And the (20A) of the (9A) came unto [Elijah], saying, **9** Arise, get thee to Zarephath, which belongeth to Zidon, and dwell there: behold, I have commanded a (12D) woman there to sustain thee. **10** So he arose and went to Zarephath. And when he came to the gate of the city, behold, the widow woman was there gathering of (11D): and he called to her, and said, Fetch me, I pray thee, a little water in a (15D), that I may (14A). **11** And as she was going to (13A) it, he called to her, and said, Bring me, I pray thee, a morsel of (18D) in thine hand. **12** And she said, As the Lord thy God liveth, I have not a cake, but an (10D) of meal in a barrel, and a little (5D) in a cruse: and, behold, I am gathering two sticks, that I may go in and dress it for me and my son, that we may eat it, and die. **13** And (7D) said unto her, (8A) (1D); go and do as thou hast said: but make me thereof a little (17A) first, and bring it unto me, and after make for thee and for thy son. **14** For thus saith the Lord God of (3D), The (21A) of meal shall not waste, neither shall the (16D) of oil fail, until the day that the Lord sendeth (2A) upon the earth. **15** And she went and did according to the saying of Elijah: and she, and he, and her (10A), did eat many days. **16** And the barrel of meal (6A) not, neither did the cruse of oil fail, according to the word of the Lord, which he spake by Elijah.

33. JONAH

Jonah 2

Then Jonah prayed unto the LORD his God out of the fish's (14A), **2** And said, I cried by reason of mine (10D) unto the LORD, and he heard me; out of the belly of hell cried I, and thou heardest my voice. **3** For thou hadst cast me into the (16A), in the midst of the seas; and the (1D) compassed me about: all thy billows and thy (7D) passed over me. **4** Then I said, I am cast out of thy (8D); yet I will look again toward thy (2D) (13D). **5** The waters compassed me about, even to the soul: the (4D) closed me round about, the (12D) were wrapped about my head. **6** I went down to the bottoms of the (5A); the earth with her bars was about me for ever: yet hast thou brought up my life from corruption, (3A/2W) my God. **7** When my soul fainted within me I remembered the LORD: and my (6A) came in unto thee, into thine holy temple. **8** They that observe lying (15A) forsake their own (20A). **9** But I will sacrifice unto thee with the voice of (9A); I will pay that that I have vowed. (11D) is of the LORD. **10** And the LORD spake unto the fish, and it (17A) out Jonah upon the (18D) (19A).

34. PARABLE OF THE TALENTS

Matthew 25:14–15, 19–29

For the kingdom of heaven is as a man travelling into a far country, who called his own servants, and delivered unto them his goods. **15** And unto one he gave five (4D), to another two, and to another one; to every man according to his several ability; and straightway took his (21A)....**19** After a long time the lord of those servants cometh, and reckoneth with them. **20** And so he that had received five talents came and brought other five talents, saying, (15A), thou deliveredst unto me five talents: behold, I have gained beside them (13A) talents more. **21** His lord said unto him, (19A) (9A), thou good and faithful servant: thou hast been (6D) over a few things, I will make thee ruler over many (10A): enter thou into the joy of thy lord. **22** He also that had received two talents came and said, Lord, thou deliveredst unto me two talents: behold, I have gained two other talents beside them. **23** His lord said unto him, Well done, good and faithful (11D); thou hast been faithful over a few things, I will make thee (16D) over many things: enter thou into the joy of thy (7A). **24** Then he which had (12D) the one talent came and said, Lord, I knew thee that thou art an (3D) man, reaping where thou hast not (1A), and gathering where thou hast not strawed: **25** And I was (18A), and went and hid thy talent in the (20A): lo, there thou hast that is thine. **26** His lord answered and said unto him, Thou (2D) and slothful servant, thou knewest that I reap where I sowed not, and gather where

I have not strawed: **27** Thou oughtest therefore to have put my (17D) to the exchangers, and then at my coming I should have received mine own with usury. **28** Take therefore the talent from him, and give it unto him which hath ten talents. **29** For unto every one that hath shall be given, and he shall have (8A): but from him that hath not shall be (14A) (5A) even that which he hath.

35. PARABLE OF THE SOWER

Matthew 13:3-9, 18-23

Behold, a sower went forth to sow; **4** And when he (11A), some seeds fell by the way side, and the (10D) came and devoured them up: **5** Some fell upon (2A) (9A), where they had not much earth: and forthwith they (11D) (8D), because they had no deepness of (13D): **6** And when the sun was up, they were (4D); and because they had no root, they withered away. **7** And some fell among thorns; and the thorns sprung up, and (1D) them: **8** But other fell into good ground, and brought forth (10A), some an hundredfold, some sixtyfold, some thirtyfold. **9** Who hath ears to hear, let him hear. . . . **18** Hear ye therefore the parable of the sower. **19** When any one heareth the word of the (16A), and understandeth it not, then cometh the (12A) (6D), and catcheth away that which was sown in his heart. This is he which received (4A) by the way side. **20** But he that received the seed into stony places, the same is he that heareth the word, and anon with (15D) receiveth it; **21** Yet hath he not (17A) in himself, but dureth for a while: for when (3D) or persecution ariseth because of the word, by and by he is (7A). **22** He also that received seed among the thorns is he that heareth the word; and the care of this world, and the deceitfulness of (5A), choke the word, and he becometh (14A). **23** But he that received seed into the good ground is he that heareth the word, and understandeth it; which also beareth fruit, and bringeth forth, some an hundredfold, some sixty, some thirty.

36. PARABLE OF THE PRODIGAL SON

Luke 15:11-24

11 And he said, A certain man had (21A) (5D): **12** And the younger of them said to his father, Father, give me the portion of goods that falleth to me. And he divided unto them his living. **13** And not many days after the (7A) son gathered all together, and took his (9D) into a far country, and there wasted his substance with (4D) (16D). **14** And when he had spent all, there arose a mighty (19A) in that land; and he began to be in (18D). **15** And he went and joined himself to a citizen of that country; and he sent him into his fields to feed (20A). **16** And he would fain have filled his (15A) with the husks that the swine did eat: and no man gave unto him. **17** And when he came to himself, he said, How many hired (12A) of my father's have bread enough and to spare, and I perish with (11A)! **18** I will arise and go to my father, and will say unto him, Father, I have (10A) against (1D), and before thee, **19** And am no more worthy to be called thy son: make me as one of thy (11D) servants. **20** And he arose, and came to his father. But when he was yet a great way off, his father saw him, and had compassion, and ran, and fell on his neck, and (6D) him. **21** And the son said unto him, Father, I have sinned against heaven, and in thy sight, and am no more worthy to be (3A) (13D/2W). **22** But the father said to his servants, Bring forth the best (2D), and put it on him; and put a (8D) on his hand, and shoes on his (17D): **23** And

bring hither the fatted calf, and kill it; and let us eat, and be (14A): **24** For this my son was dead, and is alive again; he was lost, and is found. And they began to be merry.

37. JESUS HEALS MANY

Luke 8:43–48; 17:11–19

And a woman having an issue of (15A) twelve years, which had spent all her living upon physicians, neither could be healed of any, **44** Came behind him, and touched the border of his (10A): and immediately her issue of blood stanched. **45** And Jesus said, (6D) (16A) (12A)? When all denied, Peter and they that were with him said, (11D), the multitude throng thee and press thee, and sayest thou, Who touched me? **46** And Jesus said, Somebody hath touched me: for I perceive that (14D) is gone out of me. **47** And when the woman saw that she was not hid, she came (1A), and falling down before him, she declared unto him before all the people for what cause she had touched him, and how she was (9D) immediately. **48** And he said unto her, (17A), be of good comfort: thy faith hath made thee whole; go in peace.

And it came to pass, as he went to Jerusalem, that he passed through the midst of Samaria and (3D). **12** And as he entered into a certain village, there met him ten men that were (8A), which stood afar off: **13** And they lifted up their (4D), and said, Jesus, Master, have (2D) on us. **14** And when he saw them, he said unto them, Go shew yourselves unto the (5D). And it came to pass, that, as they went, they were (13D). **15** And one of them, when he saw that he was healed, turned back, and with a loud voice glorified God, **16** And fell down on his face at his

feet, giving him thanks: and he was a Samaritan. **17** And Jesus answering said, Were there not ten cleansed? but where are the (19A)? **18** There are not found that returned to give (7A) to God, save this (18A). **19** And he said unto him, Arise, go thy way: thy faith hath made thee (6A).

38. THE HOLY SPIRIT ARRIVES

Acts 2:1-8, 12-21

And when the day of Pentecost was fully come, they were all with one accord in one place. **2** And suddenly there came a sound from heaven as of a rushing (7D) (17D), and it filled all the house where they were sitting. **3** And there appeared unto them cloven tongues like as of (18A), and it sat upon each of them. **4** And they were all filled with the (14A) (10A), and began to speak with other (11D), as the Spirit gave them utterance. **5** And there were dwelling at Jerusalem Jews, devout men, out of every nation under (14D). **6** Now when this was noised abroad, the multitude came together, and were confounded, because that every man heard them speak in his own (15A). **7** And they were all amazed and marvelled, saying one to another, Behold, are not all these which speak Galilaeans? **8** And how hear we every man in our own tongue, wherein we were (19A)? . . . **12** And they were all amazed, and were in (2D), saying one to another, What meaneth this? **13** Others mocking said, These men are full of new wine. **14** But Peter, standing up with the (12D), lifted up his voice, and said unto them, Ye men of (1D), and all ye that dwell at Jerusalem, be this known unto you, and hearken to my words: **15** For these are not (5A), as ye suppose, seeing it is but the third hour of the day. **16** But this is that which was spoken by the prophet Joel; **17** And it shall come to pass in the (13D) (3A), saith God, I will pour out of my (8A) upon all flesh: and your sons and your daughters shall prophesy, and

your young men shall see visions, and your old men shall dream (3D): **18** And on my servants and on my handmaidens I will pour out in those days of my Spirit; and they shall prophesy: **19** And I will shew wonders in heaven above, and signs in the earth beneath; (4D), and fire, and vapour of (6A): **20** The sun shall be turned into darkness, and the (9D) into blood, before the great and notable day of the Lord come: **21** And it shall come to pass, that whosoever shall call on the name of the Lord shall (16A) (6D).

39. JESUS' BIRTH

Luke 2:1-20

And it came to pass in those days, that there went out a (19A) from Caesar Augustus that all the world should be taxed. **2** (And this taxing was first made when Cyrenius was governor of Syria.) **3** And all went to be (18A), every one into his own city. **4** And (16D) also went up from Galilee, out of the city of (14A), into Judaea, unto the city of David, which is called Bethlehem; (because he was of the house and lineage of (4A):) **5** To be taxed with Mary his espoused wife, being great with (7D). **6** And so it was, that, while they were there, the days were accomplished that she should be delivered. **7** And she brought forth her (1A) son, and wrapped him in swaddling clothes, and laid him in a (10D); because there was no room for them in the inn. **8** And there were in the same country shepherds abiding in the field, keeping watch over their (11A) by night. **9** And, lo, the angel of the Lord came upon them, and the glory of the Lord shone round about them: and they were sore (15D). **10** And the angel said unto them, (6A) (17A): for, behold, I bring you good tidings of great joy, which shall be to all (13D). **11** For unto you is born this day in the city of David a (2D), which is Christ the Lord. **12** And this shall be a sign unto you; Ye shall find the babe wrapped in swaddling (12D), lying in a manger. **13** And suddenly there was with the angel a multitude of the heavenly (9A) praising God, and saying, **14** (8A) to God in the highest, and on earth peace, good will toward men. **15** And it

came to pass, as the angels were gone away from them into heaven, the shepherds said one to another, Let us now go even unto (5D), and see this thing which is come to pass, which the Lord hath made known unto us. **16** And they came with haste, and found (10A), and Joseph, and the babe lying in a manger. **17** And when they had seen it, they made known abroad the saying which was told them concerning this child. **18** And all they that heard it wondered at those things which were told them by the shepherds. **19** But Mary kept all these things, and pondered them in her (3D). **20** And the shepherds returned, glorifying and praising (20D) for all the things that they had heard and seen, as it was (21A) unto them.

40. JESUS DEDICATED AT THE TEMPLE

Luke 2:25–39

25 And, behold, there was a man in Jerusalem, whose name was (15A); and the same man was just and (13D), waiting for the consolation of Israel: and the (14A) (4A) was upon him. **26** And it was revealed unto him by the Holy Ghost, that he should not see death, before he had seen the Lord's (5A). **27** And he came by the Spirit into the temple: and when the (11D) brought in the child Jesus, to do for him after the custom of the (8A), **28** Then took he him up in his arms, and blessed God, and said, **29** Lord, now lettest thou thy servant depart in peace, according to thy word: **30** For mine eyes have seen thy (6D), **31** Which thou hast prepared before the face of all people; **32** A light to lighten the Gentiles, and the glory of thy people (3D). **33** And Joseph and his mother marvelled at those things which were spoken of him. **34** And Simeon blessed them, and said unto (10A) his mother, Behold, this (5D) is set for the fall and rising again of many in Israel; and for a sign which shall be spoken against; **35** (Yea, a sword shall pierce through thy own (1D) also,) that the thoughts of many hearts may be (9A). **36** And there was one Anna, a prophetess, the daughter of Phanuel, of the tribe of Aser: she was of a great age, and had lived with an (12A) seven years from her virginity; **37** And she was a (2A) of about fourscore and four years, which departed not from the (17A), but served God with fastings and (16A) night and day. **38** And she coming in that instant gave (7D) likewise unto the

Lord, and spake of him to all them that looked for redemption in Jerusalem. **39** And when they had performed all things according to the law of the Lord, they returned into (4D), to their own city Nazareth.

41. THE WISE MEN

Matthew 2:1-12

Now when Jesus was born in Bethlehem of Judaea in the days of (20A) the king, behold, there came wise men from the east to Jerusalem, **2** Saying, Where is he that is born (13D) of the (17D)? for we have seen his (4D) in the (7A), and are come to worship him. **3** When Herod the king had heard these things, he was (1D), and all Jerusalem with him. **4** And when he had gathered all the chief (11D) and scribes of the people together, he demanded of them where (21A) should be born. **5** And they said unto him, In Bethlehem of Judaea: for thus it is written by the (8A), **6** And thou Bethlehem, in the land of Juda, art not the least among the (9D) of Juda: for out of thee shall come a Governor, that shall (6D) my people Israel. **7** Then Herod, when he had privily called the (14A) (3D), enquired of them diligently what time the star appeared. **8** And he sent them to Bethlehem, and said, Go and search diligently for the young child; and when ye have found him, bring me word again, that I may come and (15D) him also. **9** When they had heard the king, they departed; and, lo, the star, which they saw in the east, went before them, till it came and stood over where the (18A) child was. **10** When they saw the star, they (12A) with exceeding great joy. **11** And when they were come into the (16D), they saw the young child with Mary his mother, and fell down, and worshipped him: and when they had opened their (19A), they presented unto him gifts; (10A),

and frankincense and (5A). **12** And being warned of God in a (2A) that they should not return to Herod, they departed into their own country another way.

42. YOUNG JESUS TEACHES AT THE TEMPLE

Luke 2:40–52

And the child (17A), and waxed strong in spirit, filled with (15A): and the grace of God was upon him. **41** Now his (7D) went to Jerusalem every year at the feast of the passover. **42** And when he was (2D) years old, they went up to Jerusalem after the custom of the feast. **43** And when they had fulfilled the days, as they returned, the child Jesus tarried behind in Jerusalem; and (14D) and his mother knew not of it. **44** But they, supposing him to have been in the company, went a day's journey; and they sought him among their kinsfolk and acquaintance. **45** And when they found him not, they turned back again to (10D), seeking him. **46** And it (8A) to (18A), that after three days they found him in the (12A), sitting in the midst of the doctors, both hearing them, and asking them questions. **47** And all that heard him were astonished at his (3D) and answers. **48** And when they saw him, they were (13D): and his mother said unto him, (9A), why hast thou thus dealt with us? behold, thy (1A) and I have sought thee sorrowing. **49** And he said unto them, How is it that ye sought me? wist ye not that I must be about my Father's (11D)? **50** And they understood not the saying which he spake unto them. **51** And he went down with them, and came to Nazareth, and was subject unto them: but his (6A) kept all these sayings in her (5A). **52** And Jesus increased in wisdom and (16A), and in favour with God and (4A).

43. JESUS TURNS WATER INTO WINE

John 2:1–11

And the third day there was a (1A) in Cana of Galilee; and the mother of Jesus was there: **2** And both (16A) was called, and his disciples, to the marriage. **3** And when they wanted (12D), the (13D) of Jesus saith unto him, They have no wine. **4** Jesus saith unto her, (12A), what have I to do with thee? mine hour is not yet come. **5** His mother saith unto the servants, Whatsoever he saith unto you, (5A/2W). **6** And there were set there (9A) waterpots of (15A), after the manner of the purifying of the Jews, containing two or three firkins apiece. **7** Jesus saith unto them, Fill the waterpots with (10A). And they filled them up to the (3D). **8** And he saith unto them, Draw out now, and bear unto the governor of the (4D). And they bare it. **9** When the (11A) of the feast had tasted the water that was made wine, and knew not whence it was: (but the (9D) which drew the water knew;) the (2D) of the feast called the bridegroom, **10** And saith unto him, Every man at the beginning doth set forth good wine; and when men have well (8D), then that which is worse: but thou hast kept the (7A) wine until now. **11** This beginning of (6A) did Jesus in (14A) of Galilee, and manifested forth his (7D); and his disciples (3A) on him.

44. JESUS CALLS SIMON PETER

Luke 5:1–11

And it came to pass, that, as the people pressed upon him to hear the (3D) of (13A), he stood by the lake of Gennesaret, **2** And saw two (10A) standing by the lake: but the fishermen were gone out of them, and were washing their (1A). **3** And he entered into one of the ships, which was Simon's, and prayed him that he would thrust out a little from the land. And he sat down, and (8A) the people out of the ship. **4** Now when he had left speaking, he said unto (2D), Launch out into the (18A), and let down your nets for a draught. **5** And Simon answering said unto him, (12D), we have toiled all the night, and have taken (7D): nevertheless at thy word I will let down the net. **6** And when they had this done, they inclosed a great multitude of (5D): and their net brake. **7** And they beckoned unto their partners, which were in the other ship, that they should come and help them. And they came, and (4D) both the ships, so that they began to (9A). **8** When Simon (11D) saw it, he fell down at Jesus' knees, saying, Depart from me; for I am a sinful man, (14D/2W). **9** For he was astonished, and all that were with him, at the draught of the fishes which they had taken: **10** And so was also James, and (16A), the sons of Zebedee, which were partners with Simon. And (15A) said unto Simon, (4A) not; from henceforth thou shalt catch (17A). **11** And when they had brought their ships to (6A), they forsook all, and (5A) him.

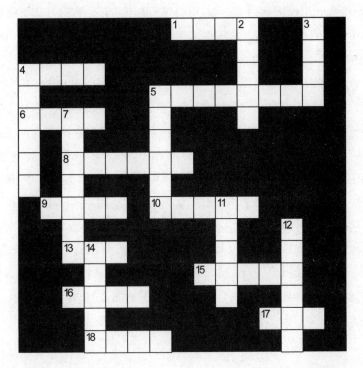

45. ZACCHAEUS

Luke 19:2–10

And, behold, there was a man named Zacchaeus, which was the (15A) among the (8D), and he was (18D). **3** And he sought to see Jesus who he was; and could not for the press, because he was (3D) of stature. **4** And he ran before, and climbed up into a (14D) tree to see him: for he was to pass that way. **5** And when (10A) came to the place, he looked up, and saw him, and said unto him, Zacchaeus, make (16D), and come down; for to day I must abide at thy (7A). **6** And he made haste, and came down, and received him (10D). **7** And when they saw it, they all (1D), saying, That he was gone to be guest with a man that is a (4A). **8** And Zacchaeus stood, and said unto the Lord: Behold, Lord, the half of my (13A) I give to the (9D); and if I have taken any thing from any man by (2D) accusation, I restore him (2A). **9** And Jesus said unto him, This day is (11D) come to this house, forsomuch as he also is a (6D) of (17A). **10** For the Son of man is come to (19A) and to (12D) that which was (5A).

46. PAUL AND SILAS IN PRISON

Acts 16:25–36

And at (2D) Paul and Silas prayed, and (14A) praises unto God: and the prisoners heard them. **26** And suddenly there was a great (3D), so that the foundations of the prison were shaken: and immediately all the (15D) were opened, and every one's bands were loosed. **27** And the keeper of the (20A) awaking out of his (4A), and seeing the prison doors (16D), he drew out his (1D), and would have killed himself, supposing that the (5D) had been fled. **28** But Paul cried with a (6A) voice, saying, Do thyself no (17D): for we are all here. **29** Then he called for a light, and sprang in, and came (7A), and fell down before Paul and Silas, **30** And brought them out, and said, Sirs, what must I do to be (11A)? **31** And they said, Believe on the Lord Jesus Christ, and thou shalt be saved, and thy (9A). **32** And they spake unto him the word of the Lord, and to all that were in his house. **33** And he took them the same hour of the (12D), and washed their stripes; and was (10D), he and all his, straightway. **34** And when he had brought them into his house, he set (18A) before them, and rejoiced, believing in (8D) with all his house. **35** And when it was day, the magistrates sent the serjeants, saying, Let those men go. **36** And the (13D) of the prison told this saying to Paul, The magistrates have sent to let you go: now therefore depart, and go in (19A).

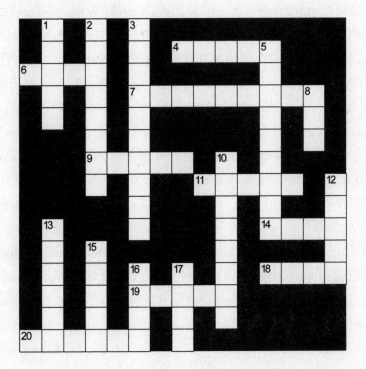

47. JESUS RAISES LAZARUS FROM THE DEAD

John 11:20-27, 32-35, 41-44

Then Martha, as soon as she heard that Jesus was coming, went and met him: but Mary sat still in the house. **21** Then said (14D) unto Jesus, Lord, if thou hadst been here, my brother had not died. **22** But I know, that even now, whatsoever thou wilt ask of (1D), God will give it thee. **23** Jesus saith unto her, Thy (9A) shall rise again. **24** Martha saith unto him, I know that he shall (16A) again in the resurrection at the last (15D). **25** Jesus said unto her, I am the (2D), and the life: he that believeth in me, though he were (15A), yet shall he live: **26** And whosoever liveth and believeth in me shall never die. Believest thou this? **27** She saith unto him, Yea, Lord: I believe that thou art the (17A), the Son of God, which should come into the (4D). . . . **32** Then when Mary was come where Jesus was, and saw him, she fell down at his (10A), saying unto him, Lord, if thou hadst been here, my brother had not (3A). **33** When Jesus therefore saw her weeping, and the (11A) also (13D) which came with her, he groaned in the (12D), and was troubled. **34** And said, Where have ye laid him? They said unto him, Lord, come and see. **35** Jesus (13A). . . . **41** Then they took away the (8D) from the place where the dead was laid. And Jesus lifted up his eyes, and said, Father, I thank thee that thou hast (5D) me. **42** And I knew that thou hearest me always: but because of the people which stand by I said it, that they may believe that thou hast

sent me. **43** And when he thus had spoken, he cried with a loud voice, (7A), come forth. **44** And he that was dead came forth, bound (5A) and foot with graveclothes: and his face was bound about with a napkin. Jesus saith unto them, (6A) him, and let him go.

48. THE WOMAN AT THE WELL

John 4:5–7, 9–11, 13–19, 25–26, 28–30

Then cometh [Jesus] to a city of Samaria. . . . **6** Now Jacob's
well was there. (6A) therefore, being wearied with his journey,
sat thus on the well: and it was about the sixth hour. **7** There
cometh a (2A) of Samaria to draw (8A): Jesus saith unto her,
Give me to drink. . . . **9** Then saith the woman of (16A) unto
him, How is it that thou, being a (6D), askest drink of me, which
am a woman of Samaria? for the Jews have no dealings with
the Samaritans. **10** Jesus answered and said unto her, If thou
knewest the (5A) of (17A), and who it is that saith to thee, Give
me to drink; thou wouldest have asked of him, and he would
have given thee (1D) water. **11** The woman saith unto him, Sir,
thou hast nothing to (11D) with, and the well is deep: from
whence then hast thou that living water? . . . **13** Jesus answered
and said unto her, Whosoever drinketh of this water shall thirst
again: **14** But whosoever drinketh of the water that I shall give
him shall never (15D); but the water that I shall give him shall
be in him a (14A) of water springing up into everlasting (4D).
15 The woman saith unto him, Sir, give me this water, that I
thirst not, neither come hither to draw. **16** Jesus saith unto her,
Go, call thy (13D), and come hither. **17** The woman (3D) and
said, I have no husband. Jesus said unto her, Thou hast well said,
I have no husband: **18** For thou hast had (7A) husbands; and
he whom thou now hast is not thy husband: in that saidst thou
(10D). **19** The woman saith unto him, Sir, I perceive that thou

art a (12A). . . . **25** I know that Messias cometh, which is called (9A): when he is come, he will tell us all things. **26** Jesus saith unto her, I that speak unto thee am he. . . . **28** The woman then left her (18A), and went her way into the (9D), and saith to the men, **29** Come, see a man, which told me all things that ever I did: is not this the Christ? **30** Then they went out of the city, and came unto him.

49. JESUS CALMS THE STORM

Mark 4:35–41

35 And the same (14A), when the even was come, he saith unto them, Let us pass over unto the other (1D). **36** And when they had sent away the (8D), they took him even as he was in the (16D). And there were also with him other (2D) ships. **37** And there arose a great (7A) of wind, and the (3D) beat into the ship, so that it was now (17A). **38** And he was in the hinder part of the ship, asleep on a (13D): and they awake him, and say unto him, (19A), carest thou not that we (18A)? **39** And he arose, and rebuked the (3A), and said unto the sea, (6A), be (1A). And the wind ceased, and there was a great (5A). **40** And he (4D) unto them, Why are ye so (9D)? how is it that ye have no (12D)? **41** And they feared exceedingly, and said one to (15A), What (11D) of man is this, that even the wind and the (10A) obey him?

50. PETER WALKS ON WATER

Matthew 14:22-33

22 And straightway Jesus constrained his (7D) to get into a ship, and to go before him unto the other side, while he sent the multitudes away. **23** And when he had sent the multitudes away, he went up into a mountain apart to (14D): and when the evening was come, he was there (15A). **24** But the ship was now in the midst of the (1A), tossed with (2D): for the wind was contrary. **25** And in the fourth watch of the (18D) Jesus went unto them, walking on the sea. **26** And when the disciples saw him walking on the sea, they were troubled, saying, It is a (11A); and they cried out for (10D). **27** But straightway Jesus spake unto them, saying, Be of good (21A); it is I; be not (19A). **28** And Peter answered him and said, Lord, if it be thou, bid me come unto thee on the (16D). **29** And he said, Come. And when (22A) was come down out of the (1D), he walked on the water, to go to (9A). **30** But when he saw the wind boisterous, he was afraid; and beginning to (17A), he cried, saying, Lord, (5A) (3D). **31** And immediately Jesus stretched forth his (13D), and caught him, and said unto him, O thou of little (12A), wherefore didst thou (8D)? **32** And when they were come into the ship, the wind ceased. **33** Then they that were in the ship came and (6A) him, saying, Of a truth thou art the (4D) of (20A).

51. THE GOOD SAMARITAN

Luke 10:25–37

And, behold, a certain (2D) stood up, and tempted him, saying, Master, what shall I do to inherit eternal life? **26** He said unto him, What is written in the (4A)? how readest thou? **27** And he answering said, Thou shalt (4D) the Lord thy God with all thy heart, and with all thy soul, and with all thy (11D), and with all thy mind; and thy neighbour as thyself. **28** And he said unto him, Thou hast answered right: this do, and thou shalt live. **29** But he, willing to justify himself, said unto Jesus, And who is my neighbour? **30** And Jesus answering said, A certain man went down from Jerusalem to (9D), and fell among thieves, which stripped him of his raiment, and wounded him, and departed, leaving him half (10A). **31** And by chance there came down a certain (12D) that way: and when he saw him, he passed by on the (5A) side. **32** And likewise a (7A), when he was at the place, came and looked on him, and passed by on the other side. **33** But a certain (3A), as he journeyed, came where he was: and when he saw him, he had compassion on him, **34** And went to him, and bound up his (17A), pouring in oil and wine, and set him on his own (1D), and brought him to an (15A), and took (14D) of him. **35** And on the morrow when he departed, he took out two pence, and gave them to the (18A), and said unto him, Take care of him; and whatsoever thou spendest more, when I come again, I will (6D) thee. **36** Which now of these three, thinkest thou, was neighbour unto him that fell among the (8D)? **37** And he said, He that shewed (13A) on him. Then said Jesus unto him, Go, and do thou (16A).

52. JESUS FEEDS 5,000

Matthew 14:14–21

And Jesus went forth, and saw a (15D) multitude, and was moved with (18A) toward them, and he healed their (16D). **15** And when it was evening, his (4A) came to him, saying, This is a (12D) place, and the time is now past; send the multitude away, that they may go into the (11D), and buy themselves victuals. **16** But (3D) said unto them, They need not (4D); give ye them to (17A). **17** And they say unto him, We have here but (5D) loaves, and two (7A). **18** He said, Bring them hither to me. **19** And he commanded the (13A) to sit down on the grass, and took the five (14A), and the (10A) fishes, and looking up to (2D), he blessed, and brake, and gave the loaves to his disciples, and the disciples to the multitude. **20** And they did all eat, and were filled: and they took up of the fragments that remained (8A) baskets full. **21** And they that had eaten were about (1D) (6D) men, beside (9D) and children.

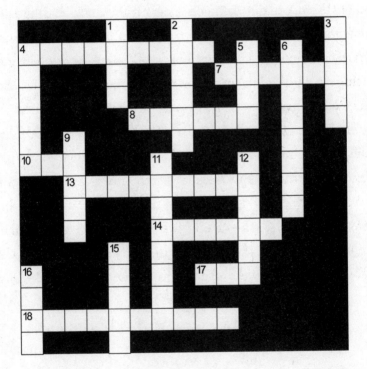

53. JESUS HEALS THE PARALYZED MAN
Mark 2:1–12

And again he entered into (8D) after some days; and it was noised that he was in the house. **2** And straightway many were gathered together, insomuch that there was no (10D) to receive them, no, not so much as about the door: and he (1A) the word unto them. **3** And they come unto him, bringing one (7A) of the palsy, which was borne of four. **4** And when they could not come nigh unto him for the press, they uncovered the (14D) where he was: and when they had broken it up, they let down the (15A) wherein the sick of the (1D) lay. **5** When Jesus saw their (9A), he said unto the sick of the palsy, Son, thy sins be (9D) thee. **6** But there was certain of the scribes sitting there, and reasoning in their hearts, **7** Why doth this man thus (4A) blasphemies? who can forgive (6A) but God only? **8** And immediately when Jesus perceived in his (4D) that they so reasoned within themselves, he said unto them, Why (14A) ye these things in your (2D)? **9** Whether is it easier to say to the sick of the palsy, Thy sins be forgiven thee; or to say, (3D), and take up thy bed, and (5D)? **10** But that ye may know that the Son of man hath (11A) on earth to forgive sins, (he saith to the sick of the palsy,) **11** I say unto thee, Arise, and take up thy bed, and go thy way into thine house. **12** And immediately he (13D), took up the bed, and went forth before them all; insomuch that they were all (12A), and glorified God, saying, We never saw it on this fashion.

54. THE LAST SUPPER

Matthew 26:17–30

Now the first day of the (15A) of unleavened (1D) the disciples came to Jesus, saying unto him, Where wilt thou that we prepare for thee to eat the (17A)? **18** And he said, Go into the city to such a man, and say unto him, The Master saith, My time is at hand; I will keep the passover at thy (10A) with my disciples. **19** And the (4A) did as Jesus had appointed them; and they made ready the passover. **20** Now when the even was come, he sat down with the (16D). **21** And as they did (3A), he said, Verily I say unto you, that one of you shall (12D) me. **22** And they were exceeding sorrowful, and began every one of them to say unto him, (14D), is it I? **23** And he answered and said, He that dippeth his hand with me in the (6A), the same shall betray me. **24** The (5D) of (9A) goeth as it is written of him: but (8D) unto that man by whom the Son of man is betrayed! it had been good for that man if he had not been (12A). **25** Then Judas, which betrayed him, answered and said, Master, is it I? He said unto him, Thou hast said. **26** And as they were eating, Jesus took bread, and (1A) it, and brake it, and gave it to the disciples, and said, Take, eat; this is my (19A). **27** And he took the cup, and gave thanks, and gave it to them, saying, (18A) ye all of it; **28** For this is my (13D) of the new testament, which is shed for many for the remission of (11D). **29** But I say unto you, I will not drink henceforth of this (15D) of the vine, until that day when I drink it new with you in my Father's (2D). **30** And when they had sung an (7D), they went out into the mount of Olives.

55. JESUS' FATE BEFORE PILATE

Luke 23:13-25

And Pilate, when he had called together the (8D) priests and the rulers and the people, **14** Said unto them, Ye have brought this (17A) unto me, as one that perverteth the people: and, behold, I, having examined him before you, have found no (4D) in this man touching those things whereof ye (10D) him: **15** No, nor yet (16A): for I sent you to him; and, lo, nothing worthy of (15D) is done unto him. **16** I will therefore chastise him, and (5D) him. **17** (For of necessity he must release one unto them at the feast.) **18** And they (14A) out all at once, saying, Away with this man, and release unto us Barabbas: **19** (Who for a certain sedition made in the (6D), and for murder, was cast into (11D).) **20** Pilate therefore, willing to release Jesus, spake again to them. **21** But they cried, saying, (3A) him, crucify him. **22** And he said unto them the third time, Why, what (1A) hath he done? I have found no (6A) of death in him: I will therefore chastise him, and let him go. **23** And they were instant with (2D) voices, requiring that he might be crucified. And the (7D) of them and of the chief (12A) prevailed. **24** And (9A) gave sentence that it should be as they required. **25** And he released unto them him that for sedition and murder was (8A) into prison, whom they had desired; but he delivered (13D) to their will.

56. JESUS' CRUCIFIXION

Luke 23:26, 32–46

And as they led him away, they laid hold upon one (18D), a Cyrenian, coming out of the country, and on him they laid the cross, that he might bear it after Jesus. . . . **32** And there were also two other, malefactors, led with him to be put to (8A). **33** And when they were come to the place, which is called (1D), there they crucified him, and the malefactors, one on the right hand, and the other on the (14A). **34** Then said Jesus, (15D), forgive them; for they (7D) not what they do. And they parted his raiment, and cast lots. **35** And the people stood beholding. And the rulers also with them derided him, saying, He saved others; let him (5A) himself, if he be (16D), the chosen of God. **36** And the soldiers also mocked him, coming to him, and offering him (12D), **37** And saying, If thou be the (17A) of the Jews, save thyself. **38** And a superscription also was written over him in letters of Greek, and Latin, and Hebrew, THIS IS THE KING OF THE (3D). **39** And one of the malefactors which were hanged railed on him, saying, If thou be Christ, save thyself and us. **40** But the other answering (11D) him, saying, Dost not thou fear God, seeing thou art in the same condemnation? **41** And we indeed justly; for we receive the due reward of our (21A): but this man hath done nothing amiss. **42** And he said unto Jesus, Lord, remember me when thou comest into thy (9A). **43** And Jesus said unto him, Verily I say unto thee, Today shalt thou be with me in (4A). **44** And it was about the sixth hour,

and there was a darkness over all the earth until the (2D) hour. **45** And the sun was darkened, and the (6D) of the temple was rent in the midst. **46** And when (13D) had cried with a loud voice, he said, Father, into thy (20A) I commend my (19A): and having said thus, he gave up the (10D).

57. JESUS' RESURRECTION
Luke 24:1–14

Now upon the first day of the (16D), very early in the (1D), they came unto the sepulchre, bringing the spices which they had prepared, and certain others with them. **2** And they found the (2A) rolled away from the sepulchre. **3** And they entered in, and found not the body of the Lord Jesus. **4** And it came to pass, as they were much perplexed thereabout, behold, (7D) men stood by them in shining (18A): **5** And as they were (5D), and bowed down their (11D) to the earth, they said unto them, Why seek ye the (14D) among the dead? **6** He is not here, but is (12D): remember how he spake unto you when he was yet in Galilee, **7** Saying, The (2D) of (9A) must be delivered into the hands of (10A) men, and be crucified, and the (15D) day rise again. **8** And they remembered his words, **9** And returned from the sepulchre, and told all these things unto the eleven, and to all the rest. **10** It was (4A) Magdalene and Joanna, and Mary the (6A) of James, and other (16A) that were with them, which told these things unto the (13A). **11** And their words seemed to them as idle tales, and they believed them not. **12** Then arose Peter, and ran unto the sepulchre; and stooping down, he beheld the (17A) clothes laid by themselves, and departed, wondering in himself at that which was come to pass. **13** And, behold, two of them went that same day to a village called (3D), which was from Jerusalem about threescore furlongs. **14** And they (8D) together of all these things which had happened.

58. JESUS APPEARS TO THE BELIEVERS
Luke 24:15–31

And it came to pass, that, while they communed together and reasoned, Jesus himself drew near, and went with them. **16** But their (13D) were holden that they should not know him. **17** And he said unto them, What manner of (4D) are these that ye have one to another, as ye (16D), and are sad? **18** And the one of them, whose name was Cleopas, answering said unto him, Art thou only a stranger in Jerusalem, and hast not known the things which are come to pass there in these days? **19** And he said unto them, What things? And they said unto him, Concerning (12A) of Nazareth, which was a (2D) mighty in deed and (7D) before God and all the people: **20** And how the (15D) priests and our rulers delivered him to be condemned to (3D), and have (8A) him. **21** But we trusted that it had been he which should have redeemed (10D): and beside all this, to day is the third day since these things were done. **22** Yea, and certain (16A) also of our company made us astonished, which were early at the sepulchre; **23** And when they found not his (5A), they came, saying, that they had also seen a vision of (17A), which said that he was alive. **24** And certain of them which were with us went to the sepulchre, and found it even so as the women had said: but him they saw not. **25** Then he said unto them, O (9D), and slow of heart to believe all that the prophets have spoken: **26** Ought not Christ to have suffered these things, and to enter into his (6A)? **27** And beginning at Moses and

all the prophets, he expounded unto them in all the scriptures the things concerning himself. **28** And they drew nigh unto the (18A), whither they went: and he made as though he would have gone further. **29** But they constrained him, saying, Abide with us: for it is toward evening, and the day is far spent. And he went in to tarry with them. **30** And it came to pass, as he sat at meat with them, he took (14D), and blessed it, and brake, and (11A) to them. **31** And their eyes were (1A), and they knew him; and he vanished out of their sight.

59. JESUS' BAPTISM

Matthew 3

In those days came John the (7D), preaching in the wilderness of Judaea, **2** And saying, (4D) ye: for the kingdom of heaven is at (1D). **3** For this is he that was spoken of by the prophet Esaias, saying, The voice of one crying in the wilderness, Prepare ye the way of the (2D), make his paths straight. **4** And the same (5A) had his raiment of camel's hair, and a leathern girdle about his loins; and his meat was locusts and wild (14D). **5** Then went out to him Jerusalem, and all Judaea, and all the region round about Jordan, **6** And were baptized of him in (5D), confessing their sins. **7** But when he saw many of the Pharisees and Sadducees come to his baptism, he said unto them, O generation of (12A), who hath warned you to flee from the (13A) to come? **8** Bring forth therefore fruits meet for repentance: **9** And think not to say within yourselves, We have (10A) to our father: for I say unto you, that God is able of these stones to raise up children unto Abraham. **10** And now also the axe is laid unto the (6A) of the trees: therefore every tree which bringeth not forth good (18A) is hewn down, and cast into the fire. **11** I indeed (11D) you with water unto repentance. but he that cometh after me is mightier than I, whose (15A) I am not worthy to bear: he shall baptize you with the (1A) (9D), and with fire: **12** Whose fan is in his hand, and he will throughly purge his floor, and gather his (13D) into the garner; but he will burn up the chaff with unquenchable fire. **13** Then cometh Jesus from Galilee to

Jordan unto John, to be baptized of him. **14** But John forbad him, saying, I have need to be baptized of thee, and comest thou to me? **15** And Jesus answering said unto him, Suffer it to be so now: for thus it becometh us to fulfil all righteousness. Then he suffered him. **16** And Jesus, when he was baptized, went up straightway out of the (3D): and, lo, the heavens were opened unto him, and he saw the (8A) of God descending like a dove, and lighting upon him: **17** And lo a voice from heaven, saying, This is my beloved (17D), in whom I am well (16A).

60. JESUS' ASCENSION
Luke 24:36–53

And as they thus spake, Jesus himself stood in the midst of them, and saith unto them, (16D) be unto you. **37** But they were terrified and affrighted, and supposed that they had seen a spirit. **38** And he said unto them, Why are ye troubled? and why do thoughts arise in your (10A)? **39** Behold my hands and my (13A), that it is I myself: handle me, and see; for a spirit hath not flesh and (5D), as ye see me have. **40** And when he had thus spoken, he shewed them his (18A) and his feet. **41** And while they yet believed not for joy, and (3D), he said unto them, Have ye here any meat? **42** And they gave him a piece of a broiled (20A), and of an honeycomb. **43** And he took it, and did (1A) before them. **44** And he said unto them, These are the words which I spake unto you, while I was yet with you, that all things must be fulfilled, which were written in the law of (21A), and in the prophets, and in the (19A), concerning me. **45** Then opened he their understanding, that they might understand the (7D), **46** And said unto them, Thus it is written, and thus it behooved (9A) to suffer, and to rise from the dead the (2D) day: **47** And that repentance and remission of sins should be (14A) in his name among all (12D), beginning at Jerusalem. **48** And ye are witnesses of these things. **49** And, behold, I send the promise of my (6D) upon you: but tarry ye in the city of Jerusalem, until ye be endued with (4D) from on high. **50** And he led them out as far as to Bethany, and he lifted up his (15D), and blessed them.

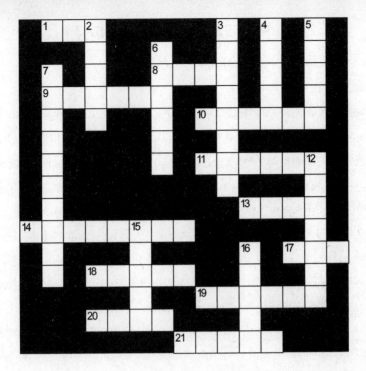

51 And it came to pass, while he blessed them, he was parted from them, and carried up into (11A). **52** And they worshipped him, and returned to Jerusalem with great (17A): **53** And were continually in the temple, praising and blessing God. (8A).

61. MARY ANOINTS JESUS' FEET

John 12:1–8

Then Jesus six days before the passover came to (9D), where Lazarus was, which had been dead, whom he raised from the (16A). **2** There they made him a (8D); and (14A) served: but (18A) was one of them that sat at the (12A) with him. **3** Then took (17A) a pound of ointment of (5D), very costly, and (6D) the feet of (7A), and wiped his feet with her (4A): and the house was (10A) with the odour of the (1A). **4** Then saith one of his disciples, Judas Iscariot, Simon's son, which should (11D) him, **5** Why was not this ointment sold for (3D) hundred pence, and given to the poor? **6** This he said, not that he cared for the poor; but because he was a (2D), and had the bag, and bare what was put therein. **7** Then said Jesus, Let her (6A): against the day of my (13D) hath she kept this. **8** For the poor (15D) ye have with you; but me ye have not always.

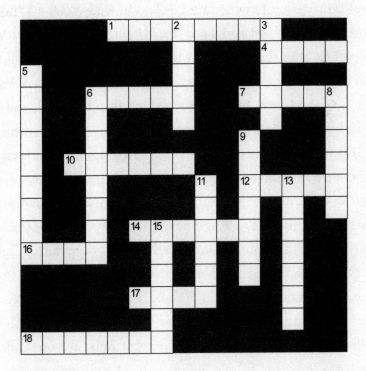

62. SAUL'S CONVERSION

Acts 9:3–18

And as [Saul] journeyed, he came near Damascus: and suddenly there shined round about him a (17D) from heaven: **4** And he fell to the (10D), and heard a voice saying unto him, (18D), Saul, why persecutest thou me? **5** And he said, Who art thou, Lord? And the Lord said, I am Jesus whom thou persecutest: it is hard for thee to kick against the pricks. **6** And he trembling and astonished said, Lord, what wilt thou have me to do? And the Lord said unto him, (19A), and go into the (6A), and it shall be told thee what thou must do. **7** And the men which (13D) with him stood speechless, hearing a (4D), but seeing no man. **8** And Saul arose from the earth; and when his eyes were opened, he saw no man: but they led him by the hand, and brought him into (3D). **9** And he was three days without (15A), and neither did eat nor drink. **10** And there was a certain disciple at Damascus, named Ananias; and to him said the Lord in a vision, Ananias. And he said, Behold, I am here, Lord. **11** And the Lord said unto him, Arise, and go into the street which is called (5A), and enquire in the house of Judas for one called Saul, of (20A): for, behold, he prayeth, **12** And hath seen in a vision a man named (11D) coming in, and putting his hand on him, that he might receive his sight. **13** Then Ananias answered, Lord, I have heard by many of this man, how much evil he hath done to thy (14A) at Jerusalem: **14** And here he hath authority from the chief priests to bind all that call on thy name. **15** But

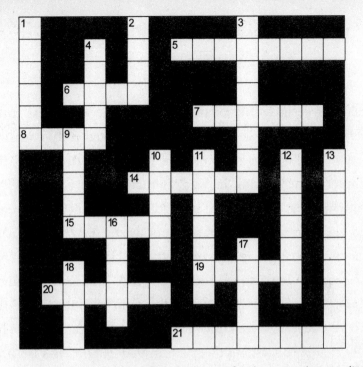

the Lord said unto him, Go thy way: for he is a chosen (7A) unto me, to bear my name before the Gentiles, and (9D), and the children of Israel: **16** For I will shew him how great things he must suffer for my name's (8A). **17** And Ananias went his way, and entered into the house; and putting his hands on him said, (12D) Saul, the Lord, even Jesus, that appeared unto thee in the way as thou camest, hath sent me, that thou mightest receive thy sight, and be filled with the (2D) (16D). **18** And immediately there fell from his eyes as it had been (1D): and he received sight forthwith, and arose, and was (21A).

63. JESUS TEMPTED BY SATAN
Matthew 4:1–11

Then was Jesus led up of the (1D) into the wilderness to be (2D) of the devil. **2** And when he had fasted forty days and forty (19A), he was afterward an hungred. **3** And when the tempter came to him, he said, If thou be the (1A) of God, command that these stones be made bread. **4** But he answered and said, It is written, Man shall not live by (6A) alone, but by every word that proceedeth out of the (12D) of God. **5** Then the (17A) taketh him up into the (14D) (18A), and setteth him on a pinnacle of the (11A), **6** And saith unto him, If thou be the Son of God, cast thyself down: for it is written, He shall give his (9A) charge concerning thee: and in their (8D) they shall bear thee up, lest at any time thou dash thy (16A) against a stone. **7** Jesus said unto him, It is written again, Thou shalt not tempt the (13D) thy God. **8** Again, the devil taketh him up into an exceeding (15D) mountain, and sheweth him all the kingdoms of the (5D), and the glory of them; **9** And saith unto him, All these things will I (10D) thee, if thou wilt fall down and (7A) me. **10** Then saith Jesus unto him, Get thee hence, (4D): for it is written, Thou shalt worship the Lord thy God, and him only shalt thou (3A). **11** Then the devil leaveth him, and, behold, angels came and ministered unto him.

64. MARY AND MARTHA

Luke 10:38–42

Now it (1A) to (11D), as they went, that he entered into a certain (17A): and a certain (9D) named (12D) received him into her (10D). **39** And she had a (8D) called (2D), which also sat at Jesus' (16D), and heard his (9A). **40** But Martha was cumbered about much (13D), and came to him, and said, (5D), dost thou not (3D) that my sister hath left me to (15A) alone? bid her therefore that she (10A) me. **41** And (7A) answered and said unto her, Martha, Martha, thou art (14A) and (4A) about many things: **42** But one (19A) is needful: and Mary hath chosen that (18D) part, which shall not be taken (6A) from her.

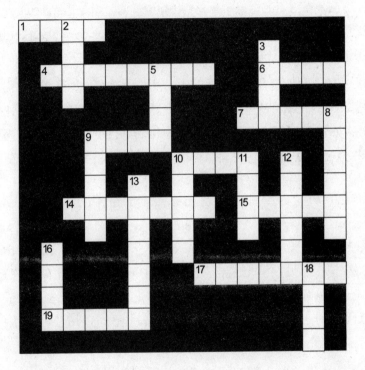

65. JUDGMENT DAY

Matthew 25:31–46

When the Son of man shall come in his (12D), and all the holy (16D) with him, then shall he sit upon the (9A) of his glory: **32** And before him shall be gathered all nations: and he shall separate them one from another, as a shepherd divideth his (18A) from the goats: **33** And he shall set the sheep on his right hand, but the goats on the (14A). **34** Then shall the (7D) say unto them on his right hand, Come, ye blessed of my Father, inherit the kingdom prepared for you from the foundation of the (4D): **35** For I was an hungred, and ye gave me (5D): I was thirsty, and ye gave me (8A): I was a stranger, and ye took me in: **36** (13D), and ye clothed me: I was sick, and ye visited me: I was in (19A), and ye came unto me. **37** Then shall the righteous answer him, saying, Lord, when saw we thee an hungred, and fed thee? or thirsty, and gave thee drink? **38** When saw we thee a stranger, and took thee in? or naked, and clothed thee? **39** Or when saw we thee (2D), or in prison, and came unto thee? **40** And the King shall answer and say unto them, Verily I say unto you, Inasmuch as ye have done it unto one of the (15A) of these my brethren, ye have done it unto me. **41** Then shall he say also unto them on the left hand, (8D) from me, ye cursed, into everlasting (6D), prepared for the (11D) and his angels: **42** For I was an hungred, and ye gave me no meat: I was thirsty, and ye gave me no drink: **43** I was a stranger, and ye took me not in: naked, and ye clothed me not: sick, and in prison, and ye visited

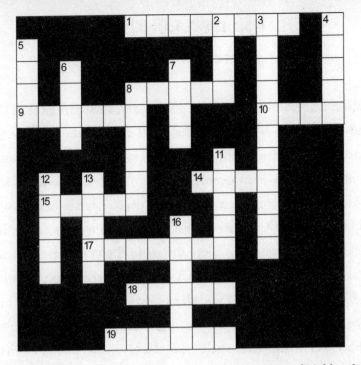

me not. **44** Then shall they also answer him, saying, (10A), when saw we thee an hungred, or athirst, or a stranger, or naked, or sick, or in prison, and did not (1A) unto thee? **45** Then shall he answer them, saying, Verily I say unto you, Inasmuch as ye did it not to one of the least of these, ye did it not to me. **46** And these shall go away into (3D) punishment: but the righteous into life (17A).

66. THE END OF THE BIBLE

Revelation 22:13–21

I am (2D) and Omega, the beginning and the (18A), the (13A) and the last. **14** Blessed are they that do his commandments, that they may have right to the (8D) of life, and may enter in through the (4D) into the city. **15** For without are dogs, and (11D), and whoremongers, and murderers, and idolaters, and whosoever loveth and maketh a lie. **16** I Jesus have sent mine (3A) to testify unto you these things in the churches. I am the (15D) and the offspring of (1A), and the bright and morning (7A). **17** And the Spirit and the bride say, Come. And let him that heareth say, (6A). And let him that is athirst come. And whosoever will, let him take the (16A) of life freely. **18** For I testify unto every man that heareth the words of the (9D) of this book, If any man shall add unto these things, God shall add unto him the plagues that are written in this book: **19** And if any man shall take away from the words of the book of this prophecy, God shall take away his part out of the book of (14A), and out of the (12A) city, and from the things which are (19A) in this book. **20** He which testifieth these things saith, Surely I come (5D). Amen. Even so, come, (14D) (10A). **21** The grace of our Lord Jesus (6D) be with you all. (17D).

67. THE TEN COMMANDMENTS

Exodus 20:1–17

And God spake all these words, saying, **2** I am the LORD thy God, which have brought thee out of the land of (8D), out of the house of bondage. **3** Thou shalt have no other (17D) before me. **4** Thou shalt not make unto thee any (1D) image, or any likeness of any thing that is in (7A) above, or that is in the (4A) beneath, or that is in the (5D) under the earth. **5** Thou shalt not bow down thyself to them, nor (20A) them: for I the LORD thy God am a (16A) God, visiting the iniquity of the fathers upon the children unto the third and fourth generation of them that hate me; **6** And shewing mercy unto thousands of them that (3D) me, and keep my commandments. **7** Thou shalt not take the name of the LORD thy God in (6A); for the LORD will not hold him guiltless that taketh his name in vain. **8** Remember the (10D) day, to keep it (11A). **9** Six days shalt thou labour, and do all thy work: **10** But the seventh day is the sabbath of the LORD thy God: in it thou shalt not do any work, thou, nor thy son, nor thy daughter, thy manservant, nor thy maidservant, nor thy cattle, nor thy stranger that is within thy (14A): **11** For in six days the LORD made heaven and earth, the sea, and all that in them is, and rested the seventh day: wherefore the LORD blessed the sabbath day, and (13D) it. **12** Honour thy father and thy (12A): that thy days may be long upon the (19A) which the LORD thy God giveth thee. **13** Thou shalt not kill. **14** Thou shalt not commit (2A). **15** Thou shalt not (15D). **16** Thou shalt

not bear (9A) witness against thy neighbour. **17** Thou shalt not (18A) thy neighbour's house, thou shalt not covet thy neighbour's wife, nor his manservant, nor his maidservant, nor his ox, nor his ass, nor any thing that is thy neighbour's.

68. PSALM 23

The (4D) is my (12D); I shall not want. **2** He maketh me to lie down in (8D) pastures: he leadeth me beside the still (13D). **3** He restoreth my (9D): he leadeth me in the paths of (17A) for his name's sake. **4** Yea, though I walk through the (19A) of the shadow of (14D), I will fear no (18D): for thou art with me; thy (6D) and thy (1A) they comfort me. **5** Thou preparest a (2D) before me in the presence of mine (16A): thou anointest my (7A) with oil; my (10A) runneth over. **6** Surely (8A) and (11A) shall follow me all the days of my (15A): and I will dwell in the (7D) of the LORD (3D) (5A).

69. THE LOVE CHAPTER
1 Corinthians 13

Though I (17D) with the tongues of men and of angels, and have not charity, I am become as sounding brass, or a tinkling (12D). **2** And though I have the gift of prophecy, and understand all (7D), and all knowledge; and though I have all faith, so that I could remove (18A), and have not charity, I am nothing. **3** And though I bestow all my (14D) to feed the poor, and though I give my body to be burned, and have not charity, it profiteth me nothing. **4** Charity suffereth long, and is kind; charity envieth not; charity vaunteth not itself, is not (4D) up, **5** Doth not (10A) itself unseemly, seeketh not her own, is not easily provoked, thinketh no (11D); **6** Rejoiceth not in iniquity, but rejoiceth in the (3D); **7** Beareth all things, believeth all things, hopeth all things, endureth all things. **8** Charity never faileth: but whether there be prophecies, they shall fail; whether there be tongues, they shall (16A); whether there be knowledge, it shall (19A) away. **9** For we know in part, and we prophesy in part. **10** But when that which is perfect is come, then that which is in part shall be done away. **11** When I was a child, I spake as a child, I understood as a (5A), I thought as a child: but when I became a (15D), I put away childish things. **12** For now we see through a glass, (13A); but then face to (8A): now I know in part; but then shall I know even as also I am known. **13** And now abideth (1D), (6D), charity, these three; but the (9D) of these is (2A).

70. LOVE (FOR OTHERS)

And this is his commandment, That we should (3D) on the name of his Son Jesus Christ, and (6A) one another, as he gave us commandment.
1 John 3:23

He that loveth his brother abideth in the (1D), and there is none occasion of stumbling in him.
1 John 2:10

Hereby perceive we the love of God, because he laid down his (18A) for us: and we ought to lay down our lives for the brethren.
1 John 3:16

Let love be without dissimulation. Abhor that which is (5D); cleave to that which is good. Be kindly affectioned one to another with (2D) love; in honour preferring one another.
Romans 12:9–10

But as (7A) brotherly love ye need not that I (17D) unto you: for ye yourselves are taught of God to love one another.
1 Thessalonians 4:9

Seeing ye have purified your souls in obeying the (8A) through the (19A) unto unfeigned love of the brethren, see that ye love one another with a (4A) heart fervently.
1 Peter 1:22

My little (13D), let us not love in (15D), neither in tongue; but in (20A) and in truth.
1 John 3:18

Beloved, let us love one another: for love is of God; and every one that loveth is (16A) of (21A), and knoweth God. He that loveth not knoweth not God; for God is (12A).
1 John 4:7–8

Put on therefore, as the elect of God, (14A) and beloved, bowels of mercies, kindness, humbleness of mind, (9D), longsuffering; Forbearing one another, and (10D) one another, if any man have a quarrel against any: even as Christ (11A) you, so also do ye.
Colossians 3:12–13

71. SALVATION

Therefore if any man be in (16A), he is a new (7A): old things are passed away; behold, all things are become new.
2 Corinthians 5:17

For he hath made him to be sin for us, who knew no sin; that we might be made the (1D) of God in him.
2 Corinthians 5:21

For this is (11D) and acceptable in the sight of God our Saviour; Who will have all men to be (9A), and to come unto the knowledge of the (6A).
1 Timothy 2:3–4

My little children, these things write I unto you, that ye sin not. And if any man sin, we have an (8D) with the Father, Jesus Christ the righteous: And he is the propitiation for our sins: and not for ours only, but also for the sins of the whole world.
1 John 2:1–2

And you, being dead in your sins and the uncircumcision of your (13A), hath he quickened together with him, having (5A) you all trespasses.
Colossians 2:13

This is a faithful saying and worthy of all acceptation. For therefore we both labour and suffer reproach, because we trust in the living God, who is the Saviour of all men, specially of those that (15A).
1 Timothy 4:9–10

But not as the offence, so also is the free (3D). For if through the offence of one many be dead, much more the (14D) of God, and the gift by grace, which is by one man, Jesus Christ, hath abounded unto many.
Romans 5:15

But after that the (10D) and love of God our Saviour toward man appeared, Not by works of righteousness which we have done, but according to his (2D) he saved us, by the washing of regeneration, and renewing of the (17A) (11A); Which he shed on us abundantly through Jesus Christ our Saviour.
Titus 3:4–6

But as many as received him, to them gave he (12D) to become the sons of God, even to them that believe on his (4D): Which were born, not of (15D), nor of the will of the (18A), nor of the will of man, but of God.
John 1:12–13

72. WISDOM

If any of you lack (12A), let him ask of God, that giveth to all men liberally, and upbraideth not; and it shall be (13D) him.
James 1:5

And he will teach us of his ways, and we will walk in his (4D).
Isaiah 2:3

I will instruct thee and (7A) thee in the way which thou shalt go: I will (13A) thee with mine eye.
Psalm 32:8

For God giveth to a man that is good in his sight (5D), and (8D), and joy.
Ecclesiastes 2:26

I will bless the LORD, who hath given me counsel: my (6A) also instruct me in the (15D) seasons.
Psalm 16:7

Then shalt thou understand the (2D) of the LORD, and find the knowledge of God. For the LORD giveth wisdom: out of his mouth cometh knowledge and (16A). He layeth up sound wisdom for the righteous: he is a buckler to them that (1D) uprightly.
Proverbs 2:5–7

Evil men understand not (10D): but they that seek the LORD understand all things.
Proverbs 28:5

And we know that the Son of God is come, and hath given us an understanding, that we may know him that is (9D), and we are in him that is true, even in his Son Jesus Christ. This is the true God, and eternal life.
1 John 5:20

For God, who commanded the (18A) to shine out of darkness, hath shined in our (14D), to give the light of the knowledge of the glory of God in the (3A) of Jesus Christ.
2 Corinthians 4:6

Happy is the man that findeth wisdom, and the man that getteth understanding. For the merchandise of it is better than the merchandise of (11A), and the gain thereof than fine (17D).
Proverbs 3:13–14

73. GRACE

Let us therefore come (3A) unto the throne of grace, that we may obtain mercy, and find grace to help in time of need.
Hebrews 4:16

For by grace are ye saved through (12D); and that not of yourselves: it is the gift of God.
Ephesians 2:8

What shall we say then? Shall we continue in sin, that grace may abound? God (15A). How shall we, that are dead to sin, (13A) any longer therein?
Romans 6:1–2

Grace be to you and (8A) from God our Father, and from the Lord (11D) Christ.
2 Corinthians 1:2

As every man hath received the (4A), even so minister the same one to another, as (14D) stewards of the manifold grace of God.
1 Peter 4:10

And he said unto me, My grace is sufficient for thee: for my strength is made (18A) in weakness. Most gladly therefore will I rather (2D) in my infirmities, that the power of Christ may rest upon me.
2 Corinthians 12:9

For all have (17A), and come short of the glory of God; Being justified (5D) by his grace through the redemption that is in Christ Jesus.
Romans 3:23–24

But grow in grace, and in the knowledge of our Lord and Saviour Jesus Christ. To him be glory both now and for ever. (9A).
2 Peter 3:18

But none of these things move me, neither count I my life dear unto myself, so that I might finish my course with (11A), and the ministry, which I have received of the Lord Jesus, to testify the (1D) of the grace of God.
Acts 20:24

For the (10A) was given by Moses, but grace and (7A) came by Jesus Christ.
John 1:17

For sin shall not have (6D) over you: for ye are not (16D) the law, but under grace.
Romans 6:14

74. FORGIVENESS

For the (9A) of sin is death; but the gift of God is (2A) life through Jesus Christ our Lord.
Romans 6:23

He hath not dealt with us after our sins; nor rewarded us according to our iniquities. For as the (15A) is high above the (10A), so great is his mercy toward them that (17D) him.
Psalm 103:10–11

If we (12D) our sins, he is (8D) and just to forgive us our sins, and to (1D) us from all unrighteousness.
1 John 1:9

And when ye stand (4A), forgive, if ye have ought against any: that your Father also which is in heaven may forgive you your trespasses. But if ye do not forgive, neither will your Father which is in heaven forgive your trespasses.
Mark 11:25–26

Then Peter said unto them, (3D), and be baptized every one of you in the name of Jesus Christ for the remission of sins, and ye shall receive the gift of the (6A) (5D).
Acts 2:38

And that repentance and remission of (18D) should be preached in his name among all (7A), beginning at Jerusalem.
Luke 24:47

For this is my (14A) of the new testament, which is (16A) for many for the remission of sins.
Matthew 26:28

Be it known unto you therefore, men and (19A), that through this man is preached unto you the forgiveness of sins.
Acts 13:38

To the (13D) our God belong (20A) and forgivenesses, though we have (11D) against him.
Daniel 9:9

75. THE SERMON ON THE MOUNT

Matthew 5:21–26, 38–48

Ye have heard that it was said of them of old time, Thou shalt not (9A); and whosoever shall kill shall be in danger of the judgment: **22** But I say unto you, That whosoever is angry with his brother without a cause shall be in danger of the judgment: and whosoever shall say to his brother, (16D), shall be in danger of the council: but whosoever shall say, Thou (18A), shall be in danger of (11A) (3D). **23** Therefore if thou bring thy gift to the altar, and there rememberest that thy brother hath ought against thee; **24** Leave there thy gift before the altar, and go thy way; first be reconciled to thy (5A), and then come and offer thy gift. **25** Agree with thine adversary quickly, whiles thou art in the way with him; lest at any time the adversary deliver thee to the judge, and the (8A) deliver thee to the officer, and thou be cast into (13D). **26** Verily I say unto thee, Thou shalt by no means come out thence, till thou hast paid the uttermost farthing. . . . **38** Ye have heard that it hath been said, An eye for an (7A), and a tooth for a (10D): **39** But I say unto you, That ye resist not (15D): but whosoever shall smite thee on thy right cheek, turn to him the other also. **40** And if any man will sue thee at the law, and take away thy (17D), let him have thy (2D) also. **41** And whosoever shall compel thee to go a (4D), go with him twain. **42** Give to him that asketh thee, and from him that would borrow of thee turn not thou away. **43** Ye have heard that it hath been said, Thou shalt (12D) thy neighbour, and (11D)

thine enemy. **44** But I say unto you, Love your enemies, (5D) them that (6D) you, do good to them that hate you, and pray for them which despitefully use you, and persecute you; **45** That ye may be the children of your (14A) which is in heaven: for he maketh his sun to rise on the evil and on the good, and sendeth rain on the just and on the (19A). **46** For if ye love them which love you, what (16A) have ye? do not even the publicans the same? **47** And if ye salute your brethren only, what do ye more than others? do not even the publicans so? **48** Be ye therefore (1A), even as your Father which is in heaven is perfect.

76. THE BEATITUDES
Matthew 5:1–16

And seeing the multitudes, he went up into a (2D): and when he was set, his disciples came unto him: **2** And he opened his mouth, and taught them, saying, **3** Blessed are the poor in spirit: for theirs is the kingdom of (18A). **4** Blessed are they that (8A): for they shall be comforted. **5** Blessed are the (2A): for they shall inherit the earth. **6** (11D) are they which do hunger and thirst after righteousness: for they shall be (13D). **7** Blessed are the merciful: for they shall obtain (1D). **8** Blessed are the pure in heart: for they shall see (14A). **9** Blessed are the peacemakers: for they shall be called the (9D) of God. **10** Blessed are they which are persecuted for righteousness' (4A): for theirs is the kingdom of heaven. **11** Blessed are ye, when men shall revile you, and persecute you, and shall say all manner of (17A) against you falsely, for my sake. **12** (5D), and be exceeding glad: for great is your (12A) in heaven: for so persecuted they the prophets which were before you. **13** Ye are the (4D) of the earth: but if the salt have lost his savour, wherewith shall it be salted? it is thenceforth good for nothing, but to be cast out, and to be trodden under foot of men. **14** Ye are the (15A) of the world. A (7A) that is set on an hill cannot be hid. **15** Neither do men light a (6A), and put it under a bushel, but on a candlestick; and it giveth light unto all that are in the house. **16** Let your light so (10A) before men, that they may see your (16D) works, and glorify your (3D) which is in heaven.

77. JESUS' PRAYER LIFE

After this manner therefore pray ye: Our (11A) which art in (13D), Hallowed be thy name. Thy (1A) come, Thy will be done in earth, as it is in heaven. Give us this day our daily (6D). And forgive us our debts, as we forgive our debtors. And lead us not into temptation, but deliver us from (12D): For thine is the kingdom, and the (4A), and the glory, for ever. Amen.
Matthew 6:9–13

At that time Jesus answered and said, I thank thee, O Father, Lord of heaven and (8D), because thou hast hid these things from the wise and prudent, and hast revealed them unto (16A). Even so, Father: for so it seemed good in thy sight.
Matthew 11:25–26

But I have prayed for thee, that thy faith (15D) not: and when thou art converted, strengthen thy brethren.
Luke 22:32

And he was withdrawn from them about a stone's cast, and (10A) down, and prayed, Saying, Father, if thou be willing, remove this (18D) from me: nevertheless not my will, but thine, be done. And there appeared an (17A) unto him from heaven, strengthening him. And being in an agony he prayed more earnestly: and his sweat was as it were great drops of (3D) falling down to the ground.
Luke 22:41–44

Then said Jesus, Father, (7A) them; for they know not what they do.
Luke 23:34

Then they took away the (5D) from the place where the dead was laid. And Jesus lifted up his eyes, and said, Father, I thank thee that thou hast heard me. And I knew that thou hearest me always: but because of the people which stand by I said it, that they may believe that thou hast (14D) me.
John 11:41–42

Now is my soul (19A); and what shall I say? Father, save me from this (9D): but for this cause came I unto this hour. Father, (2D) thy name. Then came there a voice from heaven, saying, I have both glorified it, and will glorify it again.
John 12:27–28

78. JESUS PRAYS FOR ALL BELIEVERS

John 17:20-26

Neither (15D) I for these (17D), but for them also which shall (12D) on me through their word; **21** That they all may be (3D); as thou, Father, art in me, and I in thee, that they also may be one in us: that the world may (12A) that thou hast (1A) me. **22** And the glory which thou gavest me I have given them; that they may be one, even as (19D) are (5D): **23** I in them, and thou in me, that they may be made (11D) in one; and that the world may know that thou hast (18A) me, and hast (9D) them, as thou hast loved me. **24** (16A), I will that they also, (4A) thou hast given me, be with me where I am; that they may behold my (13D), which thou hast given me: for thou lovedst me before the (14A) of the (7D). **25** O (10D) Father, the world hath not known (2D): but I have (6A) thee, and these have known that thou hast sent me. **26** And I have declared unto them thy name, and will (8A) it: that the love (20A) thou hast loved me may be in them, and I in them.

79. PROVERBS

Pride goeth before (21A), and an haughty spirit before a fall.
Proverbs 16:18

Trust in the LORD with all thine (7A); and lean not unto thine own understanding. In all thy ways acknowledge him, and he shall direct thy (1D).
Proverbs 3:5–6

The fear of the LORD is a fountain of (9A), to depart from the snares of death.
Proverbs 14:27

The way of a fool is right in his own eyes: but he that hearkeneth unto (18A) is wise.
Proverbs 12:15

He that refuseth instruction despiseth his own (6D): but he that heareth reproof getteth understanding.
Proverbs 15:32

The name of the LORD is a strong (16A): the righteous runneth into it, and is safe.
Proverbs 18:10

Train up a (20A) in the way he should go: and when he is old, he will not (14A) from it.
Proverbs 22:6

Who can find a virtuous woman? for her price is far above (10A).
Proverbs 31:10

There is a way which seemeth (13D) unto a man, but the end thereof are the ways of (4A).
Proverbs 14:12

Iron sharpeneth iron; so a man sharpeneth the countenance of his (12A).
Proverbs 27:17

A soft answer turneth away (2D): but grievous words stir up (8D).
Proverbs 15:1

He that spareth his (17D) hateth his son: but he that loveth him chasteneth him betimes.
Proverbs 13:24

A friend loveth at all times, and a (11D) is born for adversity.
Proverbs 17:17

Favour is deceitful, and (15A) is vain: but a woman that feareth the LORD, she shall be (3D).
Proverbs 31:30

A good (19D) is rather to be chosen than great (5A), and loving favour rather than silver and gold.
Proverbs 22:1

80. PARABLES OF THE LOST SHEEP AND LOST COIN

Luke 15:1–10

Then drew near unto him all the publicans and (2D) for to hear him. **2** And the Pharisees and (1D) murmured, saying, This (17D) receiveth sinners, and eateth with them. **3** And he spake this (18A) unto them, saying, **4** What man of you, having an hundred (15A), if he lose one of them, doth not leave the (3D) and nine in the wilderness, and go after that which is (12D), until he find it? **5** And when he hath found it, he layeth it on his (13A), rejoicing. **6** And when he cometh home, he calleth together his (5A) and neighbours, saying unto them, (7A) with me; for I have found my sheep which was lost. **7** I say unto you, that likewise (10A) shall be in heaven over one sinner that repenteth, more than over ninety and nine just persons, which need no repentance. **8** Either what woman having ten pieces of (4A), if she lose one piece, doth not light a (8D), and (13D) the house, and (14D) diligently till she find it? **9** And when she hath found it, she calleth her friends and her neighbours (9D), saying, Rejoice with me; for I have found the (16A) which I had lost. **10** Likewise, I say unto you, there is joy in the presence of the (11A) of God over (6A) sinner that repenteth.

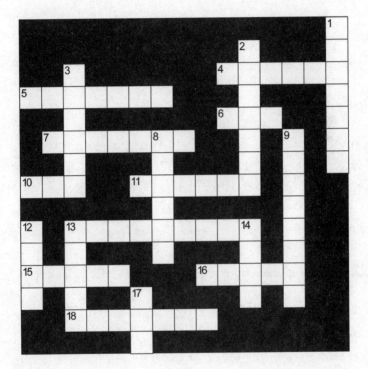

81. HEAVEN

Jesus said unto her, I am the resurrection, and the life: he that believeth in me, though he were (11A), yet shall he (15A): And whosoever liveth and believeth in me shall never (12D). Believest thou this?
John 11:25–26

And God shall wipe away all (13A) from their (16A); and there shall be no more death, neither (1D), nor crying, neither shall there be any more (3D): for the former things are passed away.
Revelation 21:4

In my Father's house are many (4A): if it were not so, I would have told you. I go to prepare a (17D) for you. And if I go and prepare a place for you, I will come (5D), and receive you unto myself; that where I am, there ye may be also.
John 14:2–3

And he shewed me a pure river of water of (10D), clear as crystal, proceeding out of the (8A) of God and of the Lamb. In the midst of the street of it, and on either side of the river, was there the tree of life, which bare twelve manner of (7D), and yielded her fruit every month: and the leaves of the tree were for the healing of the nations. And there shall be no more curse: but the throne of God and of the (15D) shall be in it; and his servants shall (6D) him: And they shall see his face; and his name shall be in their foreheads. And there shall be no night there; and they need no candle, neither light of the (2D); for the Lord God giveth them light: and they shall reign for ever and ever.
Revelation 22:1–5

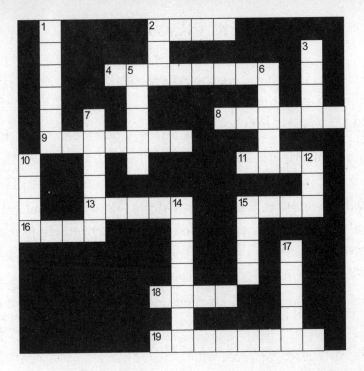

But as it is written, Eye hath not (2A), nor ear heard, neither have entered into the heart of man, the things which God hath (19A) for them that love him.
1 Corinthians 2:9

For our conversation is in heaven; from whence also we look for the (14D), the Lord Jesus Christ: Who shall change our vile (18A), that it may be fashioned like unto his glorious body, according to the (9A) whereby he is able even to subdue all things unto himself.
Philippians 3:20–21

82. THE RICH AND THE KINGDOM OF GOD

Luke 18:18–30

And a certain ruler asked him, saying, Good (16A), what shall I do to inherit eternal (9A)? **19** And Jesus said unto him, Why callest thou me (6A)? none is good, save one, that is, God. **20** Thou knowest the commandments, Do not commit (4D), Do not (1A), Do not steal, Do not bear (7D) witness, Honour thy father and thy (14A). **21** And he said, All these have I kept from my youth up. **22** Now when Jesus heard these things, he said unto him, Yet lackest thou one thing: (2D) all that thou hast, and distribute unto the (13D), and thou shalt have treasure in heaven: and come, (7A) me. **23** And when he heard this, he was very sorrowful: for he was very (11D). **24** And when (3A) saw that he was very sorrowful, he said, How hardly shall they that have riches enter into the kingdom of God! **25** For it is easier for a (5D) to go through a needle's eye, than for a rich man to enter into the (1D) of God. **26** And they that heard it said, Who then can be (15D)? **27** And he said, The things which are impossible with men are possible with God. **28** Then (12A) said, Lo, we have left all, and followed thee. **29** And he said unto them, (10A) I say unto you, There is no man that hath left house, or parents, or brethren, or (8D), or children, for the kingdom of God's (17A), **30** Who shall not receive manifold more in this present time, and in the world to come life everlasting.

83. OT PROPHECY ABOUT JESUS

Therefore the Lord himself shall give you a sign; Behold, a (6A) shall conceive, and bear a son, and shall call his (16D) Immanuel.
Isaiah 7:14

I am become a (5D) unto my brethren, and an (3D) unto my mother's children.
Psalm 69:8

He is despised and rejected of men; a man of (7A), and acquainted with grief: and we hid as it were our (1D) from him; he was despised, and we esteemed him not.
Isaiah 53:3

The Spirit of the Lord God is upon me; because the LORD hath anointed me to (11A) good tidings unto the meek; he hath sent me to bind up the brokenhearted, to proclaim liberty to the captives, and the opening of the (11D) to them that are bound; To proclaim the acceptable year of the LORD, and the day of vengeance of our God; to comfort all that (17A).
Isaiah 61:1–2

He was oppressed, and he was afflicted, yet he opened not his mouth: he is brought as a (15D) to the slaughter, and as a (8D) before her shearers is dumb, so he openeth not his mouth.
Isaiah 53:7

Therefore will I divide him a portion with the great, and he shall divide the spoil with the strong; because he hath poured out his (14A) unto death: and he was numbered with the transgressors; and he bare the sin of many, and made intercession for the transgressors.
Isaiah 53:12

For (2D) have compassed me: the assembly of the wicked have inclosed me: they pierced my (9A) and my (1A).
Psalm 22:16

Lift up your heads, O ye gates; and be ye lift up, ye everlasting doors; and the (10A) of glory shall come in. Who is this King of glory? The LORD (5A) and mighty, the LORD mighty in (18A). Lift up your heads, O ye gates; even lift them up, ye everlasting doors; and the King of glory shall come in. Who is this King of (13D)? The LORD of hosts, he is the King of glory. Selah.
Psalm 24:7–10

Thou hast ascended on (12D), thou hast led captivity captive: thou hast received (4D) for men; yea, for the rebellious also, that the LORD God might dwell among them.
Psalm 68:18

84. PRAYER

But thou, when thou prayest, enter into thy closet, and when thou hast shut thy (16A), pray to thy Father which is in (11D); and thy Father which seeth in secret shall reward thee openly.
Matthew 6:6

Confess your (7D) one to another, and pray one for another, that ye may be (9D). The effectual fervent prayer of a righteous man availeth much.
James 5:16

I will therefore that men pray every where, lifting up holy (5A), without wrath and doubting.
1 Timothy 2:8

Therefore I say unto you, What things soever ye desire, when ye pray, (10A) that ye receive them, and ye shall have them.
Mark 11:24

Continue in prayer, and watch in the same with (2A).
Colossians 4:2

Call unto me, and I will (3D) thee, and show thee (8A) and mighty things, which thou knowest not.
Jeremiah 33:3

Rejoicing in (9A); patient in tribulation; continuing (17A) in prayer.
Romans 12:12

(15A) evermore. Pray without ceasing. In every thing give thanks: for this is the (1D) of God in Christ Jesus concerning you.
1 Thessalonians 5:16–18

Evening, and morning, and at (14D), will I pray, and cry (13D): and he shall hear my voice.
Psalm 55:17

Be (4D) for nothing; but in every thing by prayer and supplication with thanksgiving let your (12A) be made known unto God. And the (6D) of God, which passeth all understanding, shall keep your hearts and (18A) through Christ Jesus.
Philippians 4:6–7

85. HUMILITY

Whosoever therefore shall humble himself as this little (7D), the same is greatest in the kingdom of (17A).
Matthew 18:4

LORD, thou hast heard the desire of the humble: thou wilt prepare their (15D), thou wilt cause thine (9A) to hear.
Psalm 10:17

Better it is to be of an humble (5A) with the lowly, than to (2D) the (18A) with the proud.
Proverbs 16:19

But he giveth more (6A). Wherefore he saith, God resisteth the proud, but giveth grace unto the humble.
James 4:6

When he maketh inquisition for (8A), he remembereth them: he forgetteth not the cry of the humble.
Psalm 9:12

By humility and the (16A) of the LORD are riches, and honour, and (13D).
Proverbs 22:4

Surely he scorneth the (11D): but he giveth grace unto the (13A).
Proverbs 3:34

The fear of the (4D) is the instruction of (10A); and before honour is humility.
Proverbs 15:33

A man's (1A) shall bring him low: but honour shall (3D) the humble in spirit.
Proverbs 29:23

Humble yourselves therefore under the (12D) hand of God, that he may (14D) you in due time.
1 Peter 5:6

86. THE CHURCH

For as we have many (9D) in one body, and all members have not the same office: So we, being many, are one (14A) in Christ, and every one members one of another.
Romans 12:4–5

For as the body is (15D), and hath many members, and all the members of that one body, being (12D), are one body: so also is (6D).
1 Corinthians 12:12

Who now (10A) in my sufferings for you, and fill up that which is (7A) of the afflictions of Christ in my (2D) for his body's sake, which is the (6A).
Colossians 1:24

And he is the (4D) of the body, the church: who is the (5A), the firstborn from the dead; that in all things he might have the preeminence.
Colossians 1:18

And hath put all things under his (2A), and gave him to be the head (8D) all things to the church.
Ephesians 1:22

For the (11D) is the head of the (3D), even as Christ is the head of the church: and he is the saviour of the body.
Ephesians 5:23

The cup of blessing which we bless, is it not the communion of the (7D) of Christ? The (16A) which we break, is it not the (1D) of the body of Christ? For we being many are one bread, and one body: for we are all (13A) of that one bread.

1 Corinthians 10:16–17

87. ANGELS

There shall no (16A) befall thee, neither shall any plague come nigh thy dwelling. For he shall give his angels (5D) over thee, to keep thee in all thy ways.
Psalm 91:10–11

Bless the Lord, ye his angels, that excel in (11A), that do his commandments, hearkening unto the voice of his (4A).
Psalm 103:20

And he shall send his angels with a great sound of a (3D), and they shall gather together his elect from the four winds, from one end of (18A) to the other.
Matthew 24:31

Be not forgetful to entertain (20A): for thereby some have entertained angels unawares.
Hebrews 13:2

And the angel of the Lord appeared unto him in a (9A) of fire out of the midst of a (6A): and he looked, and, behold, the bush burned with (13D), and the bush was not consumed.
Exodus 3:2

Take heed that ye despise not one of these (10D) ones; for I say unto you, That in heaven their angels do always behold the (14D) of my Father which is in heaven.
Matthew 18:10

Also I say unto you, Whosoever shall confess me before men, him shall the Son of man also (1D) before the angels of God: But he that denieth me before men shall be (7D) before the angels of God.
Luke 12:8–9

And suddenly there was with the angel a multitude of the heavenly (2A) praising God, and saying, (15A) to God in the highest, and on earth (19A), good will toward men.
Luke 2:13–14

In the year that king Uzziah died I saw also the LORD sitting upon a (12D), high and lifted up, and his train filled the (8A). Above it stood the seraphims: each one had six wings; with twain he covered his face, and with twain he covered his (17D), and with twain he did fly. And one cried unto another, and said, (2D), holy, holy, is the LORD of hosts: the whole earth is full of his glory.
Isaiah 6:1–3

88. PEACE

I therefore, the prisoner of the Lord, beseech you that ye walk (1D) of the vocation wherewith ye are (16A), With all lowliness and meekness, with longsuffering, forbearing one another in love; Endeavouring to keep the (8D) of the Spirit in the (17D) of peace.
Ephesians 4:1–3

Peace, peace to him that is far off, and to him that is near, saith the LORD; and I will (12D) him.
Isaiah 57:19

And let the peace of God rule in your (13A), to the which also ye are called in one (17A); and be ye thankful.
Colossians 3:15

I will (7A) what God the LORD will speak: for he will speak peace unto his people, and to his (2A).
Psalm 85:8

And the peace of God, which passeth all (16A), shall keep your hearts and (9A) through Christ (5D).
Philippians 4:7

Thy (11A) hath saved thee; go in peace.
Luke 7:50

Mark the (4D) man, and behold the upright: for the end of that man is peace.
Psalm 37:37

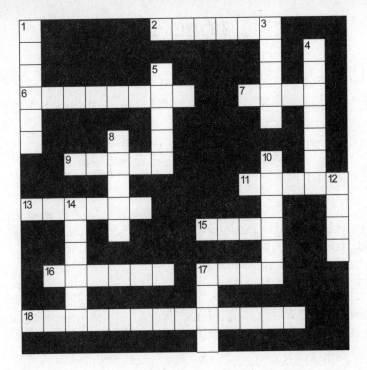

Peace I leave with you, my peace I (15A) unto you: not as the world giveth, give I unto you. Let not your heart be (6A), neither let it be (14D).
John 14:27

I will both lay me down in peace, and (3D): for thou, LORD, only makest me dwell in (10D).
Psalm 4:8

89. GOD'S WORD

(8D) and (9A) shall pass away, but my words shall not pass away.
Matthew 24:35

For I am not ashamed of the (11A) of Christ: for it is the (14D) of God unto salvation to every one that believeth.
Romans 1:16

For the word of God is quick, and powerful, and sharper than any twoedged (4D), piercing even to the dividing asunder of soul and (4A), and of the joints and marrow, and is a discerner of the thoughts and intents of the heart.
Hebrews 4:12

Search the (17A); for in them ye think ye have eternal (13D): and they are they which testify of me.
John 5:39

The entrance of thy words giveth (12D); it giveth understanding unto the simple.
Psalm 119:130

The holy scriptures. . .are able to make thee (2D) unto salvation through faith which is in Christ Jesus. All scripture is given by inspiration of God, and is profitable for (6D), for reproof, for correction, for instruction in righteousness.
2 Timothy 3:15–16

So then (16A) cometh by hearing, and hearing by the word of God.
Romans 10:17

As newborn babes, desire the sincere (1D) of the word, that ye may (11D) thereby.
1 Peter 2:2

Therefore shall ye lay up these my words in your heart and in your soul, and bind them for a sign upon your (5A), that they may be as frontlets between your eyes.
Deuteronomy 11:18

And now, brethren, I commend you to God, and to the word of his (15D), which is able to build you up, and to give you an (7D) among all them which are sanctified.
Acts 20:32

Thy word is a (13A) unto my feet, and a light unto my (3D).
Psalm 119:105

Being born again, not of corruptible seed, but of incorruptible, by the word of God, which liveth and abideth (10A/2W).
1 Peter 1:23

90. STRENGTH/COURAGE

These things I have spoken unto you, that in me ye might have (7D). In the world ye shall have tribulation: but be of good (11A); I have overcome the world.
John 16:33

Have not I (8D) thee? Be strong and of a good courage; be not (13D), neither be thou dismayed: for the LORD thy God is with thee whithersoever thou goest.
Joshua 1:9

And let us not be (4A) in well doing: for in due season we shall (6A), if we faint not.
Galatians 6:9

Be strong and of a (18A) courage, fear not, nor be afraid of them: for the LORD thy God, he it is that doth go with thee; he will not fail thee, nor (3D) thee.
Deuteronomy 31:6

Finally, my brethren, be strong in the Lord, and in the (1D) of his might.
Ephesians 6:10

And the LORD, he it is that doth go before thee; he will be with thee, he will not (12A) thee, neither forsake thee: fear not, neither be (19A).
Deuteronomy 31:8

For God hath not given us the spirit of (2D); but of power, and of (10D), and of a sound mind.
2 Timothy 1:7

Be of good courage, and he shall strengthen your heart, all ye that (14A) in the (16D).
Psalm 31:24

When thou passest through the (15A), I will be with thee; and through the rivers, they shall not overflow thee: when thou walkest through the (17A), thou shalt not be burned; neither shall the flame kindle upon thee.
Isaiah 43:2

But now thus saith the LORD that (9D) thee, O Jacob, and he that formed thee, O Israel, Fear not: for I have (5A) thee, I have called thee by thy name: thou art mine.
Isaiah 43:1

He giveth power to the (3A); and to them that have no might he increaseth strength.
Isaiah 40:29

91. GOD'S FAITHFULNESS

Know therefore that the LORD thy God, he is God, the faithful God, which keepeth covenant and (7D) with them that love him and keep his commandments to a (4D) generations.
Deuteronomy 7:9

(For the LORD thy God is a merciful God;) he will not (11A) thee, neither destroy thee, nor forget the (20A) of thy fathers which he sware unto them.
Deuteronomy 4:31

God is not a man, that he should lie; neither the (12A) of (19A), that he should (18A): hath he said, and shall he not do it? or hath he (8D), and shall he not make it good?
Numbers 23:19

If we (9D) not, yet he abideth faithful: he cannot (15A) himself.
2 Timothy 2:13

The Lord is not slack concerning his (5A), as some men count slackness; but is longsuffering to us-ward.
2 Peter 3:9

Blessed be the LORD, that hath given (10D) unto his people (14D), according to all that he promised: there hath not (11D) one word of all his good promise.
1 Kings 8:56

O Lord, thou art my God; I will (3A) thee, I will praise thy name; for thou hast done wonderful things; thy counsels of old are faithfulness and (2D).
Isaiah 25:1

And they that know thy (16A) will put their trust in thee: for thou, LORD, hast not forsaken them that (1D) thee.
Psalm 9:10

Thy word is (13A) from the beginning: and every one of thy righteous judgments endureth for ever.
Psalm 119:160

For all the promises of (6A) in him are yea, and in him (17D), unto the glory of God by us.
2 Corinthians 1:20

92. GOD'S LOVE

The LORD openeth the eyes of the (1A): the LORD raiseth them that are bowed down: the LORD loveth the (8A).
Psalm 146:8

For as a young man marrieth a (5D), so shall thy sons marry thee: and as the (6A) rejoiceth over the (16D), so shall thy God rejoice over thee.
Isaiah 62:5

The LORD thy God in the midst of thee is (7D); he will save, he will (19A) over thee with joy; he will rest in his love, he will joy over thee with singing.
Zephaniah 3:17

And we have known and (16A) the love that God hath to us. God is love; and he that dwelleth in love dwelleth in God, and God in him.
1 John 4:16

For the (13D) himself loveth you, because ye have loved me, and have believed that I came out from God.
John 16:27

I in them, and thou in me, that they may be made (3D) in one; and that the (11D) may know that thou hast (17D) me, and hast loved them, as thou hast loved me.
John 17:23

Now our Lord Jesus (10D) himself, and God, even our Father, which hath loved us, and hath given us everlasting consolation and good (18A) through (9D), Comfort your hearts, and stablish you in every (4D) word and work.
2 Thessalonians 2:16–17

For God so loved the world, that he gave his only begotten (10A), that whosoever believeth in him should not (15D), but have everlasting (14D).
John 3:16

We love him, because he (12A) loved us.
1 John 4:19

The (2D) hath appeared of old unto me, saying, Yea, I have loved thee with an everlasting love: therefore with lovingkindness have I drawn thee.
Jeremiah 31:3

93. REPENTANCE

Likewise, I say unto you, there is (15A) in the presence of the angels of God over one (20A) that repenteth.
Luke 15:10

Repent therefore of this thy (9D), and pray God, if perhaps the thought of thine (16D) may be forgiven thee.
Acts 8:22

From that time Jesus began to (11A), and to say, Repent: for the kingdom of (14A) is at hand.
Matthew 4:17

For thus saith the Lord GOD, the Holy One of Israel; In returning and (12A) shall ye be (18A); in quietness and in confidence shall be your (10D): and ye would not.
Isaiah 30:15

I came not to call the (19A), but sinners to repentance.
Luke 5:32

Repent ye therefore, and be (5D), that your sins may be (1D) out, when the times of refreshing shall come from the presence of the (6A).
Acts 3:19

Him hath God exalted with his right hand to be a (4D) and a Saviour, for to give repentance to Israel, and forgiveness of (7A).
Acts 5:31

Or despisest thou the (17D) of his goodness and forbearance and longsuffering; not knowing that the (13D) of God leadeth thee to repentance?
Romans 2:4

Take heed to yourselves: If thy brother (2D) against thee, rebuke him; and if he repent, forgive him. And if he trespass against thee (8A) times in a day, and seven times in a day turn again to thee, saying, I (3A); thou shalt forgive him.
Luke 17:3–4

94. GOD'S WILL

(16D) in the LORD with all thine (6D); and lean not unto thine own (19A). In all thy ways acknowledge him, and he shall direct thy (17A).
Proverbs 3:5–6

For I know the thoughts that I (15D) toward you, saith the LORD, thoughts of (11D), and not of evil, to give you an expected end.
Jeremiah 29:11

For this is good and acceptable in the sight of God our Saviour; Who will have all men to be (8A), and to come unto the knowledge of the (1A).
1 Timothy 2:3–4

In every thing give (2D): for this is the will of God in Christ Jesus concerning you.
1 Thessalonians 5:18

Now the God of peace, that brought again from the (3A) our Lord Jesus, that great shepherd of the (10D), through the blood of the everlasting covenant, Make you (18A) in every good work to do his will, working in you that which is wellpleasing in his sight, through Jesus Christ; to whom be (5A) for ever and ever. Amen.
Hebrews 13:20–21

And he said to them all, If any man will come after me, let him (3D) himself, and take up his (9A) daily, and follow me.
Luke 9:23

Thy kingdom come, Thy will be done in (12A), as it is in (13D).
Matthew 6:10

He hath shewed thee, O man, what is (4D); and what doth the
Lord require of thee, but to do (14D), and to love (7A), and to
walk humbly with thy God?
Micah 6:8

95. THE HOLY SPIRIT

Now the God of hope fill you with all (11D) and peace in believing, that ye may abound in (10A), through the (6D) of the Holy Ghost.
Romans 15:13

Behold, I will (2D) (16D) my spirit unto you, I will make known my (1D) unto you.
Proverbs 1:23

And I will pray the Father, and he shall give you another (15A), that he may abide with you (14D) ever; Even the Spirit of (17D); whom the (1A) cannot receive, because it seeth him not, neither knoweth him: but ye know him; for he dwelleth with you, and shall be in you.
John 14:16–17

Howbeit when he, the Spirit of truth, is come, he will (18D) you into all truth: for he shall not speak of himself; but whatsoever he shall hear, that shall he (5A): and he will shew you things to (8A).
John 16:13

If ye then, being (9D), know how to give (12A) gifts unto your (19A): how much more shall your heavenly Father give the Holy Spirit to them that ask him?
Luke 11:13

And I will put my spirit within you, and cause you to (13A) in my statutes, and ye shall keep my judgments, and do them.
Ezekiel 36:27

For the (7D) of God is not meat and drink; but (4A), and (3D), and joy in the Holy Ghost.
Romans 14:17

96. MONEY

No man can serve two (9D): for either he will (20A) the one, and (17D) the other; or else he will hold to the one, and despise the other. Ye cannot serve God and mammon.
Matthew 6:24

For the love of money is the root of all (8D): which while some coveted after, they have erred from the faith, and pierced themselves through with many (2D).
1 Timothy 6:10

And he said unto them, Take heed, and beware of covetousness: for a man's (12A) consisteth not in the (13D) of the things which he possesseth.
Luke 12:15

That they do (3D), that they be rich in good (10A), ready to distribute, willing to communicate.
1 Timothy 6:18

But to do good and to communicate forget not: for with such (4D) God is well (15A).
Hebrews 13:16

But rather give (13A) of such things as ye have; and, behold, all things are (14D) unto you.
Luke 11:41

He that hath a bountiful eye shall be (19A); for he giveth of his (11D) to the poor.
Proverbs 22:9

Every man shall (5D) as he is able, according to the blessing of the LORD thy God which he hath given thee.
Deuteronomy 16:17

Bring ye all the (1A) into the storehouse, that there may be meat in mine house, and prove me now herewith, saith the LORD of hosts, if I will not open you the (18A) of heaven, and pour you out a blessing, that there shall not be (6A) enough to receive it.
Malachi 3:10

I have shewed you all things, how that so labouring ye ought to support the (16A), and to remember the words of the Lord Jesus, how he said, It is more blessed to give than to (7A).
Acts 20:35

97. GOD'S SAFETY/PROVISION

The name of the (16A) is a strong (10A): the righteous runneth into it, and is safe.
Proverbs 18:10

The LORD shall preserve thee from all (12D): he shall preserve thy soul. The LORD shall preserve thy going out and thy coming in from this time forth, and even for (3A).
Psalm 121:7–8

When thou liest down, thou shalt not be (6D): yea, thou shalt lie down, and thy (19A) shall be sweet.
Proverbs 3:24

The (10A) of the LORD shall dwell in safety by him; and the Lord shall (18D) him all the day long, and he shall dwell between his shoulders.
Deuteronomy 33:12

Because thou hast made the LORD, which is my (4D), even the most High, thy habitation; There shall no evil befall thee, neither shall any plague come nigh thy dwelling.
Psalm 91:9–10

But whoso hearkeneth unto me shall (17D) safely, and shall be quiet from (11A) of evil.
Proverbs 1:33

I will both lay me down in (1D), and sleep: for thou, LORD, only makest me dwell in safety.
Psalm 4:8

The LORD is my (13A) and my (7D); whom shall I fear? the LORD is the strength of my life; of whom shall I be afraid?
Psalm 27:1

He maketh peace in thy (14D), and filleth thee with the finest of the (15D).
Psalm 147:14

Therefore take no thought, saying, What shall we (5A)? or, What shall we (2D)? or, Wherewithal shall we be (18A)? (For after all these things do the Gentiles seek:) for your heavenly (9A) knoweth that ye have (8A) of all these things.
Matthew 6:31–32

98. PRAISE/WORSHIP

Praise ye the LORD. Praise ye the LORD from the (7A): praise him in the heights. Praise ye him, all his (12D): praise ye him, all his (15A).
Psalm 148:1–2

O come, let us worship and (1D) (17A): let us kneel before the LORD our (10A). For he is our God; and we are the people of his pasture, and the (6D) of his hand.
Psalm 95:6–7

The four and twenty (8D) fall down before him that sat on the throne, and worship him that liveth for ever and ever, and cast their (2A) before the throne, saying, Thou art (14D), O Lord, to receive (19A) and honour and power: for thou hast (2D) all things, and for thy pleasure they are and were created.
Revelation 4:10–11

And, behold, there came a (16A) and worshipped him, saying, Lord, if thou wilt, thou canst make me (13A). And Jesus put forth his hand, and (11D) him, saying, I will; be thou clean. And immediately his (4D) was cleansed.
Matthew 8:2–3

And the four and twenty elders, which sat before God on their seats, fell upon their (18A), and worshipped God, Saying, We give thee (6D), O LORD God (5A), which art, and wast, and art to come; because thou hast taken to thee thy great (3A), and hast reigned.
Revelation 11:16–17

99. HOW TO TREAT OTHERS

But I say unto you which hear, Love your (1D), do good to them which hate you, (3D) them that curse you, and pray for them which despitefully use you. And unto him that smiteth thee on the one (17A) offer also the other; and him that taketh away thy (4A) forbid not to take thy (13A) also. Give to every man that asketh of thee; and of him that taketh away thy goods ask them not again. And as ye would that men should do to you, do ye also to them likewise. For if ye love them which (12D) you, what thank have ye? for sinners also love those that love them. And if ye do good to them which do good to you, what thank have ye? for (15A) also do even the same. And if ye (2D) to them of whom ye hope to receive, what thank have ye? for sinners also lend to sinners, to receive as much again. But love ye your enemies, and do good, and lend, hoping for (6D) again; and your (16D) shall be great, and ye shall be the children of the Highest: for he is kind unto the unthankful and to the evil. Be ye therefore (10D), as your Father also is merciful. (5D) not, and ye shall not be judged: condemn not, and ye shall not be condemned: forgive, and ye shall be (19A): Give, and it shall be given unto you; good measure, pressed down, and (11A) together, and running over, shall men give into your bosom. For with the same measure that ye mete withal it shall be measured to you again.

Luke 6:27–38

And thou shalt love the Lord thy God with all thy (6D), and with all thy (18A), and with all thy (7A), and with all thy (9A): this is the first commandment. And the second is like, namely this, Thou shalt love thy neighbour as thyself. There is none other commandment (14D) than these.

Mark 12:30–31

100. JESUS

I am he that liveth, and was dead; and, behold, I am (15A) for
evermore, Amen; and have the (16D) of hell and of death.
Revelation 1:18

He is not here: for he is (6D), as he said. Come, see the (4D)
where the Lord lay.
Matthew 28:6

In the (12A) was the Word, and the Word was with God, and
the (5A) was God. . . . And the Word was made (18A), and
dwelt among us, (and we beheld his glory, the glory as of the
only (10D) of the Father,) full of grace and (1A).
John 1:1, 14

Jesus said unto them, (14D), verily, I say unto you, Before (13D)
was, I am.
John 8:58

Let this mind be in you, which was also in Christ Jesus: Who,
being in the form of God, thought it not (8D) to be equal with
God: But made himself of no (2D), and took upon him the form
of a servant, and was made in the likeness of men: And being
found in fashion as a man, he humbled himself, and became
(9A) unto death, even the death of the cross. Wherefore God
also hath highly exalted him, and given him a name which
is above every name: That at the (17A) of Jesus every (16A)
(7A) (3D), of things in heaven, and things in earth, and things
under the earth; And that every (11D) should confess that Jesus
Christ is Lord, to the glory of God the Father.
Philippians 2:5–11

ANSWERS

1

2

3

4

5

6

7

8

9

10

11

12

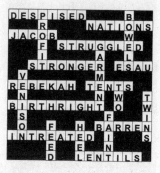

GOODLY
BECAME HERSELF
WAS HOUSE BREW
THREE HIM NURSE SISTER
MONTHS CHILD PIT
BABE CHILDREN
PHARAOH

FIRE SHOES
FATHER HOLY FLOCK
BUSH CANAANITES
JACOB ABRAHAM ISAAC LAW
HONEY MIDIAN GROUND
MOUNTAIN ANGEL MOSES
FACE AFFLICTION
EGYPT

BELIEVED CHARIOT
COVERED OVER IS
EGYPTIAN GROUND PHARAOH ISRAEL
SEASHORE EAST HAND DRY RIGHT MOSES MORNING
SAVED
LEFT HORSEMEN

BEER PROPHET SERVANT
DID AROSE
SAMUEL SHILOH
SHEBA REVEAL THIRD GREW WORD
WAX HANG LAY LORD
TEMPLE LAMB SPEAK

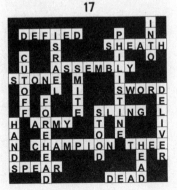

INTO
DEFIED SHEATH
CUT ISRAEL ASSEMBLY PHILISTINE
STONE MITE SWORD
OFF FOE STING DELIVER
HAND ARMY STONE THEE
CHAMPION THEE
SPEAR DEAD

PROSPERED
STONE FASTING
SIGN PALACE LIONS
DEN MORNING MOUTH
THEE FOREVER DANIEL
DELIVER BELIEVED INSTRUMENTS
EXCEEDINGLY DARIUS

31

32

33

34

35

36

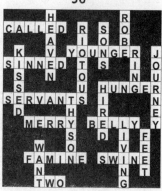

37

38

39

40

41

42

43

44

45

46

47

48

49

STILL · LITTLE · WIND · SIDE · WAVE · SAID · CALM · PEACE · STORM · F · SEA · MULTITUDE · FEARFUL · PILLOW · MAY · FAITH · ANOTHER · DAY · SHIP · PERISH · MASTER

50

SEA · W · M · SAVE · WORSHIPPED · SON · SHIP · DISCIPLE · JESUS · DOUBT · SPIRIT · FAITH · ALONE · PRAY · SINK · AFRAID · GOD · CHEER · PETER

51

SAMARITAN · LAW · LAWYER · LOVE · OTHER · REPAY · LEVITE · DEAD · MERCY · JERICHO · STRENGTH · THIEVES · CARE · PRIEST · LIKEWISE · WOUNDS · HOST

52

DISCIPLES · FISHES · JESUS · DEPART · HAVEN · THOUSAND · TWELVE · TWO · WOMEN · MULTITUDE · VILLAGE · LOAVES · DESERT · SICK · GREAT · EAT · COMPASSION

53

PREACHED · ARISE · PALSY · SPEAK · WALK · SINS · SPIRIT · SICK · FAITH · CAPERNAUM · POWER · FORGIVEN · AMAZED · ROOM · AROSE · REASON · BED · ROOF

54

BLESSED · GREAT · DISCIPLES · KINGDOM · DISH · WOE · MAN · HOUSE · BORN · BETRAY · BLOOD · FRUIT · FEAST · PASSOVER · DRINK · TWELVE · BODY

55

56

57

58

59

60

61

62

63

64

65

66

67

68

69

70

71

72

79

80

81

82

83

84

85

86

87

88

89

90

91

92

93

94

95

96

97

98

99

100

If You Like Trivia and Solving Puzzles, Here Are Two Books We Recommend

BARBOUR'S BIBLE TRIVIA ENCYLOPEDIA

Barbour's Bible Trivia Encyclopedia is perfect for trivia buffs who get excited about the names, places, geography, language, history, and other interesting factoids in scripture! This encyclopedia boasts nearly 3,000 questions to challenge the mind of every Bible scholar—multiple choice, true/false, fill-in-the-blank, open-ended questions—and more!

Paperback / 978-1-63409-308-8 / $9.99

BIBLE WORD GAMES: 150 CROSSWORDS WITHOUT CLUES

Based on the hot new Unolingo® game, this book includes 150 puzzles featuring an interlocking grid with 26 missing letters—one each from A through Z. To solve the puzzle, players must precisely insert the letters into the particular spots where they will work. . .like a letter-based Sudoku game.

Paperback / 978-1-63058-883-0 / $4.99